Writing Strategies
for the Common Core

**Integrating
Reading Comprehension
into the Writing Process**

Grades 6–8

by Hillary Wolfe

🍎 Maupin House *by*

capstone®
professional

Writing Strategies for the Common Core:
Integrating Reading Comprehension into the Writing Process, Grades 6-8
By Hillary Wolfe

Cover Design: Cynthia Akiyoshi
Book Design: Studio Montage

Image Credits:
Shutterstock: Wavebreakmedia, cover, Zakharchenko Anna, inside

Library of Congress Cataloging-in-Publication Data
Wolfe, Hillary.
Writing strategies for the common core : integrating reading comprehension
into the writing process, grades 6-8 / Hillary Wolfe.
pages cm
Includes bibliographical references and index.
ISBN 978-1-62521-524-6 (pbk. : alk. paper) 1. English language—Composition
and exercises—Study and teaching (Middle school)—United States. 2. Language
arts (Middle School)—Standards—United States. I. Title.

LB1631.W583 2013
428.0071'2—dc23

2013026793

Maupin House publishes professional resources for K-12 educators.
Contact us for tailored, in-school training or to schedule
an author for a workshop or conference.
Visit www.maupinhouse.com for free lesson plan downloads.

Maupin House Publishing, Inc. by Capstone Professional
1710 Roe Crest Drive
North Mankato, MN 56003
www.maupinhouse.com
888-262-6135
info@maupinhouse.com
10 9 8 7 6 5 4 3 2 1

Printed in the United States of America in Eau Claire, Wisconsin.
112013 007880

Table of Contents

Introduction

Research

The Common Core State Standards

During the decade before the creation of the Common Core State Standards, attention focused on effective strategies for teaching reading. Not as much attention was given to how to teach writing. Consequently, the curricula for middle-school students have been scattershot. A report to Carnegie Corporation of New York entitled "Writing Next: Effective Strategies to Improve Writing of Adolescents in Middle and High Schools" found that improving writing instruction for adolescents was "a topic that has previously not received enough attention from researchers or educators" (Graham & Perin, 2007, p. 3). However, the expectations put forth by the Common Core State Standards, in addition to the proliferation of new technology, intensified the need for instructional direction. "Writing, for adolescents who live in an age of digital communication, has taken on new importance and plays a prominent role in the way they socialize, share information, and structure their communication" (Sweeny, 2010, p. 121).

The finding was that there was still a lot of investigation that needed to be done to determine the best way to teach writing. The rich nature of the practice of writing and its relative neglect in instructional research make it inevitable that a whole compendium of possible approaches has not yet been studied. Research is clearly needed, not only to identify additional effective practices that already exist but to develop new ones (Graham & Perin, 2007, p. 26).

What was evident was that "to be successful learners, adolescent readers must master complex texts, understand the diverse literacy demands of the different content areas, and navigate digital reading" (Biancarosa, 2012, p. 22). Therefore, writing instruction, especially for adolescents, needs to be multi-purpose. "Writing instruction for adolescents may involve process writing, along with instruction in different writing forms or genres, writing conventions and grammar, evaluation and criticism, and on-demand writing with prompts or for test purposes" (Sweeny, 2010, p. 125).

Furthermore, writing is multifaceted, and as advanced technology has become more prevalent, writing has evolved to include a variety of modes of communication. "Writing is an integral part of students' lives today due to their use of texting and social networking sites, but most students do not recognize this type of communication as writing" (Sweeny, 2010, p. 124).

Balanced Literacy and Connecting Reading and Writing

The Common Core State Standards stress "the importance of the reading-writing connection by requiring students to draw upon and write about evidence from literary and informational text" (Common Core State Standards Initiative, 2011, Standards for English Language Arts, p. 8).

Allington & Gabriel (2012) also describe writing as connected to reading: "Writing provides a different modality within which to practice the skills and strategies of reading for an authentic purpose" (p. 13).

The most relevant research that has shown promise for both reading and writing instruction came from the balanced literacy model. Bitter, O'Day, et al. (2009) define balanced literacy as an approach "designed to foster the gradual release of responsibility from teachers to students, moving from structured modeling (e.g., through read-alouds and shared reading) to scaffolded support (e.g., through guided reading) to independence of individual work" (p. 27). Balanced literacy models typically combine reading and writing instruction by integrating both instruction and practice in authentic settings and for relevant purposes. This integration enriches comprehension. "Students need to learn strategies to support their comprehension, not to demonstrate the acquisition of a new skill" (Guccione, 2011, p. 575). Furthermore, research has shown that an integrated approach is preferable to a single "silver bullet" solution to literacy instruction for adolescent readers: "There is no magic bullet or one-size-fits all approach to improving adolescent literacy learning.... Current policy texts may not propose a single solution, but they do advocate a number of interventions or programs as needed reforms" (Franzak, 2006, p. 236). There are many approaches to literacy available to teachers. "Although there are many best practices for teaching students to read, the challenge is in knowing which instructional strategy to choose" (Miller & Veatch, 2010, p. 154).

Why I Wrote This Book and How to Use It

An examination of different implementation models of balanced literacy led to the creation of this curriculum. Three chapters address a text type (or genre) as defined by the Common Core State Standards for Writing—"Explanatory/Informational," "Argument," and "Narrative"—with another chapter, "Response to Literature," included because many standardized tests still contain on-demand writing that requires students to quickly respond to a poem or short narrative. "Response to Literature" is an umbrella category, in that it can encompass any of the text types. But the Common Core State Standards demand that students become accustomed to citing evidence from a piece of text and engaging in the close reading and analysis of text as part of the writing process. Chapters on the reading/writing connection and test prep round out this resource.

Within each of the three genre units, blocks of core instruction are combined to be delivered over a four- to six-week period and sample lessons were created as models for instruction. Two Mini-Lessons are included for each of three strategies per genre. The chapters on the reading/writing connection, response to literature, and test prep also contain additional strategies and Mini-Lessons. Mini-Lessons provide applicable Common Core Standards, materials lists, overviews, planning tips, procedures (including modeling, guided practice, and independent practice opportunities), reading connections, formative assessments, and reproducible graphic organizers and rubrics (both analytic for formative assessments and holistic for summative assessments).

The classroom setting for a balanced literacy model of instruction reflects constructivist principles, in which the students take more ownership of learning the strategies and skills they will need to apply across multiple content areas. "Constructivism recognizes that learning occurs most often in a social setting; thus, the formation of a classroom...is vital to student success" (Saulnier, 2008, p. 6). A classroom built to accommodate balanced literacy looks different from a traditional classroom with desks in rows. It also operates differently, as students must transition more frequently between whole-group, small-group, paired-work, and independent-work areas. Therefore, setting up the classroom and instructional plan requires a new approach. "Our teaching behaviors, our expectations we set for our students, and our students' learning behaviors must evolve to fit our students' futures" (Saulnier, 2008, p. 7).

Integrating all the components of a balanced literacy framework also requires some backward planning. The teacher must choose an overall objective and then smaller benchmark objectives that serve as prerequisites to reach the overarching goal. There also must be time for assessment (both formative and summative) and re-teaching when necessary. According to Wiggins & McTighe, learning for understanding develops in an iterative fashion across the three categories of transfer, meaning, and acquisition. The acquisition of new vocabulary [is] introduced in response to real problems...and as preparation for the final performance task...the unit culminates in a thought-provoking (and personally relevant) transfer task and a reflection on the unit's essential questions (2008, p. 38).

Structuring the Class for Balanced Literacy

According to Bitter, O'Day, et al. (2009), a balanced literacy model fosters comprehension by integrating reading and writing in both instruction and practice, in authentic settings and for relevant purposes. This approach allows for the gradual release of responsibility from teacher to student. They describe a classroom setting that offers structured modeling, scaffolded support through small-group guided practice, and opportunities for independent practice. Not only is this arrangement better suited for an integrated curriculum, it also helps promote students' self-efficacy. Swafford & Durrington (2010) explain that "the instructional practices utilized by teachers have an impact on both [self-efficacy and achievement]" (p. 222). They cite research showing that when instructional practices included teacher modeling, guided practice, and independent practice, learners were more likely to perform a new task successfully and, more importantly, were more likely to tackle and accomplish a difficult task. These practices raised self-efficacy (as cited in Bandura, 1997; Schunk, 2003; Schunk & Pajares, 2005; Schunk & Zimmerman, 2007).

Logistically, this structure presents a challenge for the middle-school classroom teacher. Average class size in California middle schools is approximately 29 students (City-Data, 2009). Students travel from class to class. Setting up and maintaining centers or workstations does not work the same way it would in an inclusive elementary classroom. Therefore, the teacher must strategize.

The following tips can help establish and streamline classroom management procedures.

Arranging the Room

Prepare your students for different group structures by teaching and practicing procedures for group arrangements.

Whole Class

Consider whether you want your students sitting in rows. Rows hinder the teacher from maintaining proximity with students, which is a key strategy for minimizing disruption. If your room allows it, consider having desks facing each other. This arrangement takes away the "back of the room" and gives the teacher quick and equal access to all students.

Consider placing desks in pods. Students in middle school respond to opportunities for social engagement, and this also gives students opportunities to practice oral language skills. "Students suggested that collaboration with a partner, small group, or the teacher would be helpful to develop oral reading confidence" (Swafford & Durrington, 2010, p. 231). Capitalize on this fact by setting up heterogeneous table groups. Each group can work as a team, and the teacher can create a reward system that encourages cooperation. Individual effort is still expected and can contribute to the success of the team. This strategy gives students ownership and responsibility for their work and can be more engaging and intrinsically motivating. Swafford & Durrington state, "To become self-efficacious readers,...students needed to experience reading in an instructional context in which they felt supported" (2010, p. 230).

Small Group

Encourage flexible grouping by instructing students how to quickly and efficiently move their desks to work in pairs, in triads, or in groups of four or five. Use symbols to represent various configurations; for example, two circles represent partner work, a triangle means they work in groups of three, a square means work in groups of four, and a five-pointed star means work in groups of five. Have students practice picking up and moving their desks to get into the appropriate formations. Be prepared to practice these configurations multiple times at first and to revisit the practice periodically through the year. Students should be expected to move their desks quickly and quietly. Once students have the procedure down pat, the teacher can simply write the appropriate symbol on the board and students will know without questioning how they are to arrange themselves for the day.

Move the station, not the students. Keep practice assignments for small-group work in laminated pocket folders or sturdy boxes or bags. Give students 10 to 15 minutes to work on one task, then move the folders or boxes to the next table. Continue working this way until all students have had a chance to complete each station's assignment. One station should be set aside for time with the teacher to address intervention or guided practice.

Independent Practice

If possible, provide some comfortable areas for students to work on their own. Beanbags, a futon in the corner, or even individual computer stations with inviting lighting will set the stage for a relaxing environment. If you must have desks in rows, tape a number to each desk and assign that number to each student. Arrange students not alphabetically, but by ability. Keep the struggling learners in front, closest to you. This will help you stay focused on those students who need more guidance and direct instruction. Be sure to rearrange students at the start of each unit so everyone has a chance to benefit from more attention from the teacher.

Using Reading and Writing Portfolios

According to Swafford & Durrington (2010), adolescents need to take ownership of their work. "There is an increasing demand on students as 21st century learners to take responsibility to continue learning outside of school, so it is extremely important for teachers to help them become self-efficacious readers" (p. 232). Using a reading and writing portfolio allows students to create their own set of reference tools, keep track of notes, and stay accountable for assignments. Here are some tips for creating and using reading and writing portfolios in class.

Be Practical

A portfolio can be as simple as six sheets of notebook paper folded in half and stapled together. Use sturdy paper to add pockets, and have students keep glue sticks in their supplies to attach handouts. A portfolio only needs to last for four weeks or as long as one unit of instruction. Have students turn in their portfolios as a form of assessment. This work product will provide more information than a report card to parents about how the student progressed through the unit.

Make a Cover Page

Let students decorate and label their portfolios as they want (within reason). Leave the first page blank so students can create a table of contents either as they go or at the end of the unit. Creating a table of contents can be a form of summarizing what they learned and can serve as a study tool. It also reinforces an understanding of features of text students need to know to read nonfiction and textbooks.

Keep the Portfolios in Class

Since these tools will be used daily, students need guaranteed access to them. Find a magazine holder or a basket and color code each one to correspond with each class period. At the beginning of class, students retrieve their portfolios, and at the end, they return them to the basket. Organize the portfolios so that all reading information is on the right side (R=right=reading) and all the writing information is on the left side. That will help students when they are trying to find information quickly.

Working Backward and Creating a Strategies Notebook

Wiggins and McTighe (2011) described a method of instructional planning that worked backward: "1) focus on teaching and assessing for understanding and learning transfer, and 2) design curriculum 'backward' from those ends" (p. 1). That is, teachers think of what they want their students to have achieved at the end of the unit and then fill in the necessary assignments and checkpoints needed to reach that goal. Each unit of instruction in this strategies notebook follows a balanced literacy framework and includes the following:

- Modeled reading instruction
- Guided reading practice
- Independent reading
- Modeled writing instruction
- Guided writing practice
- Independent writing
- Vocabulary (direct instruction of word analysis and decoding strategies)
- Content-area vocabulary (embedded in reading and writing practice)

Creating a Planning Calendar

Use the following steps to create a four-week planning calendar for teaching the strategies in this book.

Start with a Culminating Assignment

The culminating assignment for each unit reflects that specific form of writing. For example, a culminating assignment for the explanatory/informational unit could be a class newspaper, a student-authored textbook, or an essay. A culminating assignment for the argument unit could be a commercial, an editorial, or a political campaign. For the narrative unit, students could write a story, create a short video, or put on a play as a culminating experience.

The culminating assignment can also integrate content-area themes. For example, by combining mathematics and argument, students can identify a high-performing stock or bond, track its progress over a period of time, then write a letter to shareholders convincing them to buy or sell the stock. In science, students can write a narrative from the perspective of a morsel of food and describe its journey as it travels through the digestive tract. In social studies, students can write collaboratively with a partner, explaining a historical event from various perspectives.

Once the culminating assignment has been decided, write it in your planning calendar at the end of the third week. The fourth week of the unit should be saved for revisions, test preparation, and re-teaching. The summative assessment should take place in the middle of the week, so there is still time to make up work, allow students to make presentations, or revisit a skill and get ready for the next unit.

Planning Calendar 1

	Monday	Tuesday	Wednesday	Thursday	Friday
Week 1					
Week 2					
Week 3					
Week 4	Culminating Assignment Due	Presentations and Reteaching	Summative Assessment	Make Up Presentations	Make Up Presentations

Fill in Reading Instruction/Reading Practice

The purpose of a culminating assignment is to allow students to synthesize and integrate all the specific characteristics of that genre. Consider all the skills students will need to successfully master the text type. Narrow the focus to only include the most important five or six. Start the unit with an overview of the genre, and then fill in the reading instruction so that one strategy is covered every three to five days.

For example, informational text "organizes the explanation in successive steps, using imperative verbs" (Duke, Caughlan, et al., 2012, pp. 37-38). Therefore, in the explanatory unit, students will practice the following:

- Visualize while reading
- Monitor understanding by predicting
- Determine a main idea
- Distinguish a significant detail from an insignificant detail
- Summarize information

Each of these strategies will be addressed individually, as shown on the following planning calendar. Allow one or two days after the instruction for guided practice.

Fill in Writing Instruction/Writing Practice

Integrate writing into the equation and reinforce the reading and writing connection by weaving writing strategies into the calendar. This will give students opportunities to write for various purposes and time frames, as specified by the Common Core State Standards for grades six through eight: "Write routinely over extended time frames (time for research, reflection, and revision) and shorter time frames (a single sitting or a day or two) for a range of discipline-specific tasks, purposes, and audiences" (Common Core State Standards, p. 44).

For example, in the explanatory unit, if students are practicing the reading strategy of visualizing while reading, follow that lesson with a writing exercise focused on using descriptive sensory words. Give students a day after modeling to work in small groups or individually to write a descriptive piece. (See the planning calendar below.)

Planning Calendar 2

	Monday	Tuesday	Wednesday	Thursday	Friday
Week 1	RI: Visualize	RP: Guided practice	WI: Descriptive writing	WI: Descriptive writing	RI: Predict
Week 2	RP: Guided practice	WI: Cause and effect	WP: Cause and effect	RI: Main idea and detail RP: Guided practice	WI: Main idea and detail
Week 3	WP: Main idea and detail	RI: Summary	RP: Guided practice	WI: Summary Culminating assignment draft	WP: Summary Culminating assignment draft
Week 4	CA: Due	Presentations and Reteaching	Summative Assessment	Make Up Presentations	Make Up Presentations

Legend

RI = Reading Instruction
WI = Writing Instruction
RP = Reading Practice
WP = Writing Practice
CA = Culminating Assignment
ML = Mini-Lesson

Fill in Vocabulary and Grammar

Vocabulary can be addressed in a few steps. First, provide explicit and direct word analysis and decoding strategies as an opening activity two to five days each week, for 10 to 15 minutes at a time. Fill in this time on your planning calendar. Include vocabulary checks on each Friday.

Next, provide content-specific vocabulary instruction within the structure of reading and writing. This can be done as an explicit reading strategy (to look for transition words or active verbs, for example) or as a writing strategy (as part of revising and editing within the writing process). Limit vocabulary to three to five words at a time, and provide opportunities for practice through word-consciousness and word-awareness activities.

Allowing Time for Re-teaching

The final week of the unit can be saved for re-teaching, but also allow flexibility within the other weeks of the unit for a quick 20- to 30-minute review as needed. Use formative assessments regularly, and use the information gained from these tools to determine whether students are ready to move on or whether they need more scaffolded instruction. Ideas for formative assessments are included with each strategy.

Practicing Test Prep

Synthesize the unit for students and show them the relevance of the information by practicing test prep. Help students identify the key words in a prompt that will alert them as to what their response should contain. Have them practice with a few prompts at the end of the unit.

Next, show students how to use all the tools they learned throughout the unit to quickly organize a written response or to skim a reading passage for pertinent information.

Using the Mini-Lessons

The strategies in this book are organized to provide an overview of the genre or text type and then to suggest the prerequisite skills students will need before starting the unit, including the specific content vocabulary. Three strategies are introduced for segmenting the unit into three manageable pieces. These strategies correspond to the stages of the writing process—prewriting, drafting, and revising—and are meant to offer specific scaffolds as students are working through each of these stages on their way to completing a culminating assignment. Two Mini-Lessons per strategy provide specific instructional ideas for how to address those components. Finally, graphic organizers are provided as scaffolds, and rubrics for assessment are included, both analytic (for formative assessments) and holistic (for summative assessments).

Standards Correlations

The lessons in this book are correlated to the Common Core State Standards for Reading and Writing for grades six through eight.

Standards Correlations

Common Core Anchor Standards	Lesson(s)
CCSS.ELA-Literacy.CCRA.R.1 Read closely to determine what the text says explicitly and to make logical inferences from it; cite specific textual evidence when writing or speaking to support conclusions drawn from the text.	All lessons
CCSS.ELA-Literacy.CCRA.R.2 Determine central ideas or themes of a text and analyze their development; summarize the key supporting details and ideas.	All lessons
CCSS.ELA-Literacy.CCRA.R.3 Analyze how and why individuals, events, or ideas develop and interact over the course of a text.	All lessons
CCSS.ELA-Literacy.CCRA.R.4 Interpret words and phrases as they are used in a text, including determining technical, connotative, and figurative meanings, and analyze how specific word choices shape meaning or tone.	All lessons
CCSS.ELA-Literacy.CCRA.R.5 Analyze the structure of texts, including how specific sentences, paragraphs, and larger portions of the text (e.g., a section, chapter, scene, or stanza) relate to each other and the whole.	All lessons
CCSS.ELA-Literacy.CCRA.R.6 Assess how point of view or purpose shapes the content and style of a text.	All lessons
CCSS.ELA-Literacy.CCRA.R.7 Integrate and evaluate content presented in diverse media and formats, including visually and quantitatively, as well as in words.	All lessons
CCSS.ELA-Literacy.CCRA.R.8 Delineate and evaluate the argument and specific claims in a text, including the validity of the reasoning as well as the relevance and sufficiency of the evidence.	All lessons
CCSS.ELA-Literacy.CCRA.R.9 Analyze how two or more texts address similar themes or topics in order to build knowledge or to compare the approaches the authors take.	All lessons
CCSS.ELA-Literacy.CCRA.R.10 Read and comprehend complex literary and informational texts independently and proficiently.	All lessons
CCSS.ELA-Literacy.CCRA.W.1 Write arguments to support claims in an analysis of substantive topics or texts using valid reasoning and relevant and sufficient evidence.	Characteristics of Argument Text (p. 21)
CCSS.ELA-Literacy.CCRA.W.2 Write informative/explanatory texts to examine and convey complex ideas and information clearly and accurately through the effective selection, organization, and analysis of content.	Characteristics of Explanatory or Informational Text (p. 17)
CCSS.ELA-Literacy.CCRA.W.3 Write narratives to develop real or imagined experiences or events using effective technique, well-chosen details and well-structured event sequences.	Characteristics of Narrative Text (p. 25)
CCSS.ELA-Literacy.CCRA.W.4 Produce clear and coherent writing in which the development, organization, and style are appropriate to task, purpose, and audience.	All lessons
CCSS.ELA-Literacy.CCRA.W.5 Develop and strengthen writing as needed by planning, revising, editing, rewriting, or trying a new approach.	All lessons
CCSS.ELA-Literacy.CCRA.W.6 Use technology, including the Internet, to produce and publish writing and to interact and collaborate with others.	All lessons
CCSS.ELA-Literacy.CCRA.W.7 Conduct short as well as more sustained research projects based on focused questions, demonstrating understanding of the subject under investigation.	All lessons
CCSS.ELA-Literacy.CCRA.W.8 Gather relevant information from multiple print and digital sources, assess the credibility and accuracy of each source, and integrate the information while avoiding plagiarism.	How Appealing! (p. 47); Literary Devices (p. 53)
CCSS.ELA-Literacy.CCRA.W.9 Draw evidence from literary or informational texts to support analysis, reflection, and research.	Text Features and Significant Details (p. 40)
CCSS.ELA-Literacy.CCRA.W.10 Write routinely over extended time frames (time for research, reflection, and revision) and shorter time frames (a single sitting or a day or two) for a range of tasks, purposes, and audiences.	All lessons

Common Core State Standards: Writing

Grades 6–8	Lesson(s)
CCSS.ELA-Literacy.W.1 Write arguments to support claims with clear reasons and relevant evidence. **CCSS.ELA-Literacy.W.1a** Introduce claim(s) and organize the reasons and evidence clearly. **CCSS.ELA-Literacy.W.1b** Support claim(s) with clear reasons and relevant evidence, using credible sources and demonstrating an understanding of the topic or text. **CCSS.ELA-Literacy.W.1c** Use words, phrases, and clauses to clarify the relationships among claim(s) and reasons. **CCSS.ELA-Literacy.W.1d** Establish and maintain a formal style. **CCSS.ELA-Literacy.W.1e** Provide a concluding statement or section that follows from the argument presented.	Prewriting Mini-Lesson: Logical Appeals (p. 95); Prewriting Mini-Lesson: Emotional Appeals (p. 99); Drafting Mini-Lesson: Thematic Writing (p. 103); Drafting Mini-Lesson: A Strong Foundation (p. 106); Revising Mini-Lesson: Grammar (p. 111); Revising Mini-Lesson: Form and Function (p. 114); Test Prep Mini-Lesson: Argument, Determine the Task (p. 172); Test Prep Mini-Lesson: Argument, Stake Your Claim (p. 180)
CCSS.ELA-Literacy.W.2 Write informative/explanatory texts to examine a topic and convey ideas, concepts, and information through the selection, organization, and analysis of relevant content. **CCSS.ELA-Literacy.W.2a** Introduce a topic; organize ideas, concepts, and information, using strategies such as definition, classification, comparison/contrast, and cause/effect; include formatting (e.g., headings), graphics (e.g., charts, tables), and multimedia when useful to aiding comprehension. **CCSS.ELA-Literacy.W.2b** Develop the topic with relevant facts, definitions, concrete details, quotations, or other information and examples. **CCSS.ELA-Literacy.W.2c** Use appropriate transitions to clarify the relationships among ideas and concepts. **CCSS.ELA-Literacy.W.2d** Use precise language and domain-specific vocabulary to inform about or explain the topic. **CCSS.ELA-Literacy.W.2e** Establish and maintain a formal style. **CCSS.ELA-Literacy.W.2f** Provide a concluding statement or section that follows from the information or explanation presented.	Mini-Lesson: Main Ideas and Details (p. 31); Mini-Lesson: Topic and Concluding Sentences (p. 35); Prewriting Mini-Lesson: Observations (p. 61); Prewriting Mini-Lesson: Processes (p. 64); Drafting Mini-Lesson: Openings (p. 69); Drafting Mini-Lesson: Closings (p. 72); Revising Mini-Lesson: Transitional Word Choices (p. 76); Revising Mini-Lesson: Sentence Structure (p. 79); Test Prep Mini-Lesson: Explanatory/Informational, Determine the Task (p. 168); Test Prep Mini-Lesson: Explanatory/Informational, Create a Thesis (p. 176)
CCSS.ELA-Literacy.W.3 Write narratives to develop real or imagined experiences or events using effective technique, relevant descriptive details, and well-structured event sequences. **CCSS.ELA-Literacy.W.3a** Engage and orient the reader by establishing a context and introducing a narrator and/or characters; organize an event sequence that unfolds naturally and logically. **CCSS.ELA-Literacy.W.3b** Use narrative techniques, such as dialogue, pacing, and description, to develop experiences, events, and/or characters. **CCSS.ELA-Literacy.W.3c** Use a variety of transition words, phrases, and clauses to convey sequence and signal shifts from one time frame or setting to another. **CCSS.ELA-Literacy.W.3d** Use precise words and phrases, relevant descriptive details, and sensory language to convey experiences and events. **CCSS.ELA-Literacy.W.3e** Provide a conclusion that follows from the narrated experiences or events.	Prewriting Mini-Lesson: Point of View and Context (p. 129); Prewriting Mini-Lesson: Conflicts and Events (p. 134); Drafting Mini-Lesson: Rich, Relatable Characters (p. 139); Drafting Mini-Lesson: Allusions (p. 142); Revising Mini-Lesson: Repetition (p. 149); Revising Mini-Lesson: Dialogue and Voice (p. 152); Test Prep Mini-Lesson: Narrative—Determine the Task (p. 174); Test Prep Mini-Lesson: Narrative—Create Context and a Point of View (p. 184)
CCSS.ELA-Literacy.W.9 Draw evidence from literary or informational texts to support analysis, reflection, and research. **CCSS.ELA-Literacy.W.9a** Apply grade 6 Reading standards to literature (e.g., "Compare and contrast texts in different forms or genres [e.g., stories and poems; historical novels and fantasy stories] in terms of their approaches to similar themes and topics"). **CCSS.ELA-Literacy.W.9b** Apply grade 6 Reading standards to literary nonfiction (e.g., "Trace and evaluate the argument and specific claims in a text, distinguishing claims that are supported by reasons and evidence from claims that are not").	All lessons
CCSS.ELA-Literacy.W.10 Write routinely over extended time frames (time for research, reflection, and revision) and shorter time frames (a single sitting or a day or two) for a range of discipline-specific tasks, purposes, and audiences.	All lessons

Chapter 1

The Reading/ Writing Connection

Overview: Understanding Text Types and Purposes

Why connect reading and writing through instruction? A recent report to Carnegie Corporation of New York, *Writing to Read,* identified "instructional practices shown to be effective in improving students' reading" (Graham & Hebert, 2010, p. 5). The report recommended that students write about what they read, learn and practice the steps of the writing process, and write for extended periods of time.

This strategy section aims to provide a road map for choosing reading materials that will support the specific skills and structures of each particular writing genre. By practicing writing in a genre and understanding the characteristics of that genre, students will recognize those characteristics when they read. More important, they will recognize the characteristics across content areas, increasing their comprehension in other subjects.

The first step in this process is to recognize the features and characteristics of each of the three text types outlined in the Common Core State Standards:

- Explanatory or Informational Text
- Argument
- Narrative

Explanatory text is the first text type addressed because it is the most objective form of writing. The characteristics are easy to identify in multiple contexts and content areas, and the skills needed to write effective informational text are straightforward. By starting with explanatory text, students get a chance to feel successful with a writing task that feels very doable, and the personal emotional risk of writing is minimized. (Note: Some special-ed students should not be asked to write explanatory text first, as the structure may prove to be too difficult for them.)

Explanatory text is also the most prevalent kind of text students will encounter outside of school. Technical documents, applications, and resumes are just some of the examples of the kind of text that students will encounter, both as a reader and as a writer.

Finally, informational text is easily assessed, because it lends itself to a more formulaic structure. Teachers can ease into using an analytic rubric by assessing very specific elements. Similarly, students can serve as peer reviewers when they have a very clear set of criteria by which to judge another student's writing.

Mini-Lesson: Characteristics of Explanatory or Informational Text

Common Core State Standard

Write informative/explanatory texts to examine a topic and convey ideas, concepts, and information through the selection, organization, and analysis of relevant content. Produce clear and coherent writing in which the development, organization, and style are appropriate to task, purpose, and audience.

Materials

- Colored paper cut into 4" x 4" squares
- Instructions for folding an origami frog
- Advertisements showing two similar products of different brands
- Pinwheels
- Chart paper
- *Explain That!* activity sheet, page 19
- *Text Types and Purposes Reference Sheet,* page 20

Overview

Students will be introduced to characteristics and types of explanatory writing. They will begin a reference document to help them remember the characteristics and use the characteristics to help determine the purpose of informational writing.

Planning

Look for advertisements from newspapers or magazines that show two like items with different brands as a means of comparison.

Procedure

Modeling

1. Tell students they will be learning about explanatory writing. Place students into one of three groups, and distribute one sheet of chart paper to each group. Have students draw a large triangle Venn shape on their chart paper

2. Write the words *explanatory and informational* on the board, and have students write those words above the triangle Venn on their chart paper. Ask whether students recognize any smaller words or similar words within those words (*explain, inform*). Tell students that explanatory or informational text explains something.

3. Display a passage of explanatory text (how-to instructions) and ask students what this text is explaining. How did they know? Have them write some of the characteristics of how-to text on the top triangle on their chart.

4. Display a short passage of text that explains a cause-effect relationship. Ask students what this text is explaining, and tell them to write some of the characteristics of this text on the lower right triangle on their chart.

5. Display a short passage that compares two items. Ask students what this text is explaining, and tell them to write some of the characteristics of this text on the bottom left triangle on their chart.

Guided Practice

6. Distribute a copy of the *Explain That!* activity sheet to each student. Tell students that each group will be given a task. They are to work together to complete the task and then fill out the activity sheet.

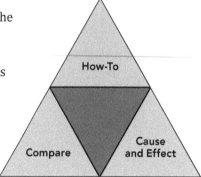

7. Distribute colored paper and origami instructions to the students in the first group. Have the second group look at the advertisements. Give pinwheels to the third group.

8. The activity sheet asks students to investigate their item/object/instructions and then explain it. Allow students about 10 minutes to fill out their activity sheets. Give each group one sheet of chart paper, and ask them to draw another triangle Venn shape. Have them label the center triangle *Purposes of Explanatory Text.* (Students will start using this chart in step 10.)

9. Ask the group with the origami frog to describe their task. Students should explain that their task involved following step-by-step instructions to build an origami frog.

10. Have one student from each group write *To Know How* in the top triangle section on the chart paper. Brainstorm with the class some more characteristics of the task (possible responses might include *step by step, clear directions, or describes how something happens or works*).

11. Ask the group with the pinwheels to describe their object. Students should explain how a pinwheel works.

12. Have one student from each group write *To Know Why* in the bottom right triangle section on the chart paper. Brainstorm with the class some more characteristics of the task (possible responses might include *why it happens, the cause, or the reason*).

13. Ask the group with the advertisements to explain their task. Students should describe which product had a better ad.

14. Have one student from each group write *To See a Relationship* in the bottom left triangle section on the chart paper. Brainstorm with the class some of the characteristics of the task (possible responses might include *to see which is better or to make a choice*).

15. Tell students they have just described the three types of informational or explanatory text.

Independent Practice

16. Post students' charts and distribute one copy of the *Text Types and Purposes Reference Sheet* to each student. In the first column, ask students to write *to explain how, to explain why,* and *to explain a relationship* in the row next to *Purpose.*

17. Tell students the first thing we do as readers is determine the purpose of the text. The purpose of informational or explanatory text will be one of the three phrases they just wrote down.

18. Have students work individually or with partners to fill in the *Features* row of the same column. Guide students to write things such as *sequential, specific details,* and *clear descriptions.*

19. Introduce the following vocabulary words to students and have them list these words in the *Vocabulary* row in the same column: *transitions, organization.*

20. Distribute a copy of nonfiction explanatory text to partners. Ask them to read the text together and find examples of the features and vocabulary from their reference chart. Then, have partners decide which purpose is being addressed by this text.

21. Have students write an explanation in their own words of explanatory or informational text. Require them to use the new vocabulary words.

Characteristics of Explanatory or Informational Text

Name: _____

Explain That!

Directions: Your group has been given an item or task. Circle the item or task for your group, and then follow the instructions for your item or task below.

(circle one)   Origami frog   Pinwheel   Advertisements

Origami:

Follow the instructions to make an origami frog. After your frog is complete, write a description of what you did. Be prepared to explain the process to your classmates.

_____

_____

_____

_____

Pinwheel:

Investigate what causes the pinwheel to spin. Write your ideas and be prepared to explain to your classmates.

_____

_____

_____

_____

Advertisements:

Study the products in the ads. Decide which is the better purchase. Write your decision and be prepared to explain your choice to your classmates.

_____

_____

_____

_____

Characteristics of Explanatory or Informational Text

Name: _____

Text Types and Purposes Reference Sheet

	Informational/ Explanatory	Argument	Narrative
Purpose			
Features			
Vocabulary			

Mini-Lesson: Characteristics of Argument Text

Common Core State Standard

Write arguments to support claims with clear reasons and relevant evidence. Produce clear and coherent writing in which the development, organization, and style are appropriate to task, purpose, and audience.

Materials

- Chart paper
- Heavy cardstock
- *Text Types and Purposes Reference Sheet,* page 20
- *Persuasive Technique Cards* (one set of six cards per group), page 23
- *Situation Cards* (one set of 6 cards per group), page 24

Overview

Students will be introduced to characteristics and types of argument text. They will continue to fill out the reference document to help them remember the characteristics and use the characteristics to help determine the types of argument writing.

Planning

Copy the *Situation* activity cards template and the *Persuasive Technique* cards template onto heavy cardstock to create enough decks of cards so that each group of four students has six Situation cards and six *Persuasive Technique* cards.

Procedure

Modeling

1. Introduce to students vocabulary that you will be using for the lesson: *rational, emotional.* Ask students for examples of when they see these terms in real life. Ask students to describe the difference between the two terms. Write their ideas on chart paper and post in the front of the room.

2. Tell students they will be playing a game and working in groups of four. The rules of the game are as follows:

   a. A stack of six *Situation* cards is placed facedown in the center of the table.

   b. Each student is given one *Persuasive Technique* card. Place the remaining *Technique* cards facedown in the center of the table. A *Persuasive Technique* card states the technique on the front and offers a more explicit description on the back. (Take time to go over the descriptions to be sure that all students understand and can ask questions before the game begins.)

   c. The game begins with one person as the judge. The judge turns over the top *Situation* card for the group to read.

   d. The *Situation* card states the role that the judge will play and lists a situation that the other players are trying to persuade the judge to take on. For example, the *Situation* card may say, "Friend. Convince your friend to join or quit a club with you."

   e. The judge for the round is the person whom each player must "convince," but each player must use his or her persuasive technique to do so. For example, a student with the persuasive technique of bandwagon might tell the judge, "You should quit the club because everyone else we know is quitting."

f. Each student will have thirty seconds to use his or her technique to convince the judge. After all students have tried, the judge will determine who was the most persuasive and award that player the *Situation* card.

g. All players hand their *Technique* card to the person on their right, and the role of the judge rotates one person to the right as well. The person who "won" the round places his or her *Technique* card in the center of the table and chooses a new *Technique* card from the deck.

h. Play continues until all players have had a chance to be the judge. The student who collects the most *Situation* cards is the winner.

Guided Practice

3. Allow students between fifteen and twenty minutes to complete the game. Walk around and facilitate as needed by answering questions about the techniques.

4. After the game is over, ask students to reflect with a partner on the game.

5. Tell students to take out their *Text Types and Purposes Reference Sheet*. Ask students what they think is the purpose of argument and write it in the first row of the second column (*to convince or persuade*).

6. In the next row of the same column, have students write *persuasive technique*. Tell students that the techniques they used (*bandwagon, logical, emotional, data/statistics, expert testimony, association*) are only a few of the ways authors try to be persuasive. Argument writing also relies on understanding your audience so you can choose the right tone and the appropriate language and words. Have students add *audience* and *word choice* in the *Features* row of their *Text Types and Purposes Reference Sheet*.

7. Have students add the vocabulary (*rational, emotional*) to the box in the third row

Independent Practice

8. Have students write answers to the following questions in their Reading Portfolios:

a. Why did the role of the judge matter? (This speaks to audience and how audience influences the tone and language of our persuasive argument.)

b. Which types of persuasive techniques were most effective? Why do you think so?

c. Which types of persuasive techniques were least effective? Why do you think so?

9. Optional extension: Ask students to find examples of different persuasive techniques in magazines, in newspapers, or on television. Have them bring in samples of what they find and display them around the room.

Characteristics of Argument Text

Persuasive Technique Cards (front)

Logical	Emotional	Data/statistics
Bandwagon	Expert testimony	Association

Persuasive Technique Cards (back)

Follow a step-by-step argument that is very rational and fact-based. (e.g., "It gets dark by 7 p.m., and I want you to be home before dark, so you need to be home before 7 p.m.")	Appeal to the other person's fear, anger, love, patriotism, or other strong feeling. (e.g., "Pit bulls can be dangerous and may attack your children, so protect yourself with this fence.").	Use charts, graphs, or other statistical information to make your point. (e.g., "Eighty percent of people who ate this vegetable lost weight.")
Make the person believe that he or she will be "left out" if he or she doesn't agree with you. (e.g., "All the popular people are wearing orange shoelaces. You should buy orange shoelaces too.")	Use words or examples from reliable "experts," such as a doctor, a police officer, or another authority figure. (e.g., "More doctors prefer this medication than other brands.")	Show how the person's actions will ultimately put him or her in an enviable position. (e.g., "If you buy the sports car, you'll be attractive and attractive people will want to be with you.")

Characteristics of Argument Text

Situation Cards

Role: Friend Situation: Convince your friend to join or quit a club with you.	Role: Parent Situation: Convince your parent to get a snake as a pet.	Role: Parent Situation: Convince your parent to let you stay out past curfew.
Role: Younger sibling (or cousin) Situation: Convince your younger sibling or cousin to go to bed.	Role: Neighbor Situation: Convince your neighbor to cut a low tree branch so you can skateboard on the sidewalk.	Role: Teacher Situation: Convince your teacher to shorten the homework assignment.

Mini-Lesson: Characteristics of Narrative Text

Common Core State Standard

Write narratives to develop real or imagined experiences or events using effective technique, relevant descriptive details, and well-structured event sequences. Produce clear and coherent writing in which the development, organization, and style are appropriate to task, purpose, and audience.

Materials

- Chart paper
- *Text Types and Purposes Reference Sheet,* page 20
- *Facebook Page* activity sheet, page 27
- *Tweet It!* activity sheet, page 28

Overview

Students will be introduced to characteristics of narrative writing. They will complete their reference document to help them remember the characteristics and use the characteristics to help determine the purpose of narrative writing.

Planning

Choose characters either from history or the news that students are familiar with, or let them invent their own characters. Make enough copies of the *Facebook Page Activity Sheet* for every student.

Procedure

Modeling

1. Tell students that today they will be learning about the characteristics of narrative text. Explain that a narrative has a specific structure and contains specific features, just like the other text types they have worked with so far.

2. Introduce the vocabulary words *sequence* and *conflict.*

3. Explain to students that if they are using a social-networking site such as Facebook, then they are participating in narrative writing already.

4. Ask students to brainstorm some of the features of a Facebook page posting. (Possible responses include *profile or description of the person, relationship status, where he or she lives, who his or her friends are, timeline, and the news feed, which describes the day-to-day happenings of the person.*) Write students' ideas on chart paper and display in the front of the room.

5. Create categories that label the parts of the Facebook page: *Who, What, Where, When, Why.*

Guided Practice

6. Distribute copies of the *Facebook Page* and *Tweet It!* activity sheets to students. Tell students they are to create a posting for a historical figure or a character from a story.

7. Have students fill in all the characteristics listed on the *Facebook* activity sheet, including at least three events on the news feed portion.

8. Ask students to share their page with one person in the class.

9. After all students have shared their page with a partner, each student will use the *Tweet It!* activity sheet to describe his or her partner's character. The *Tweet It!* activity sheet requires them to summarize the information in 10 lines or less. Students should be sure that their "tweets" include information from each of the categories described in step 4.

10. Have several students share their *Tweet It!* activity sheet summaries.

Independent Practice

11. Ask students to take out their *Text Types and Purposes Reference Sheet*.

12. In the first row of the third column of the reference sheet, have students write the purpose of a narrative (possible responses include *to tell a story or to relate a series of events*).

13. In the second row of the column, ask students to write the features of a narrative (possible responses include *who, what, where, when, and why*).

14. Have students write the vocabulary words in the last row of the column. Explain that in addition to following a sequence of events, narratives often include a conflict that drives the story by giving the character something to overcome or accomplish.

15. For a fun extension, have students narrate their "posting" and share their narratives online.

Characteristics of Narrative Text

Name:_____

Facebook Page

Directions: Choose a character from history or from a fictional book you are reading. Fill out all the character's information on this Facebook Page template.

Profile:

Timeline:

Friends:

News feed:

Characteristics of Narrative Text

Name:_____

Tweet It!

Directions: In 10 lines or less, write a tweet about the Facebook page presented to you by your partner. Include all elements of a narrative, including who, what, where, when, and why.

_____

_____

_____

_____

_____

_____

_____

_____

_____

_____

Overview: Writing from the Inside Out

When someone asks for directions to get somewhere, it's easier to provide him or her with a detailed map if you've actually made the trip yourself. You are able to quickly determine the important landmarks or road signs to watch for, and can get that person to his or her destination as quickly as possible with minimal distractions. But if you've never been there yourself, all you can offer is a general idea of where to go, without really giving the kind of key information your traveler needs to be confident about the route.

The same is true for writing. When students try to write an essay by first focusing on the introduction, it's like trying to draw a map to a place they've never been. Yet that is what is asked of students all the time. They are expected to start with an introduction that describes their topic and then come up with a thesis—their opinion about the topic—including three or more reasons why they feel that way. Then they are to write their body paragraphs to support their thesis. This seems so backward! Imagine trying to give a route to a place you've never been!

Ideas don't occur in ready-made order. Students need to experience the stages of the writing process in which they brainstorm, put their ideas down, and then start to sort and organize them into some kind of order that makes sense. They could sort their ideas from most important to least important, or they could follow a sequential order. They could be writing to solve a problem, in which case they would want to explain the problem first and then offer several good solutions. In this case, they might want to save their best solution for last. Perhaps they are arguing for or against something. In this case, they would want to offer counterarguments along the way.

When students follow the steps of the writing process, they find that they are really writing from the inside out. They are putting their strongest ideas down on paper, then using strategies and tools to organize and sort those ideas. Then, they can get feedback from others (peers or teachers) and revise their ideas, their organization, and even specific word choices. They may need to find more evidence to support their ideas, which may in turn influence their organization.

After students have spent some time manipulating their words and have settled on a structure, then they will be ready to make their road map.

The introduction serves to tell the reader what he or she is about to encounter. It starts with a hook that engages the reader and then follows up with a description of what the reader can expect to find in the text. Then, the introduction outlines the format and the key points of interest, so the reader knows what to look for and anticipates these transitions as he or she is reading.

If the student has already determined the structure and the key points, then writing the introduction is easy. The student only has to use his or her own paper as the reference document. But without this reference, the student is making it up and hoping the ideas that follow will actually match the introduction.

Start students out by determining how to distinguish relevant from unimportant details in a text. Once they know how to offer strong support for a main idea, they'll be on their way to creating an organized paper. Then, have students go back and write their introduction. Finally, have them write a closing that mirrors the introduction and sums up the journey that the reader took. The closing is almost like a memory book, offering souvenirs and mementos from the trip and reaffirming everything that was presented in the introduction.

You may have heard of this process before, described in this way:

- "Tell them what you're going to tell them."
- "Tell them."
- "Tell them what you told them."

Students may think this approach is a little strange at first, but ultimately, it takes a lot of pressure off. They find that it is easier to throw out all kinds of ideas and then winnow down to only their best thoughts. Then, when students write their introductions, they aren't overwhelmed by the prospect of what to write or how to start.

This section provides a Mini-Lesson for identifying and writing main ideas and details. Then, it introduces topic and concluding sentences as a way to provide structure to a paragraph. The last lesson gives students a chance to practice doing research so they understand the importance of using primary and secondary sources when doing research.

Mini-Lesson: Main Ideas and Details

Common Core State Standard

Develop the topic with relevant facts, definitions, concrete details, quotations, or other information and examples.

Materials

- Three different colored sticky notes or note cards (one set for each student)
- Chart paper
- Short nonfiction text
- *Text Types and Purposes Reference Sheet,* page 20
- *Main Ideas and Details* activity sheet, page 33
- Paper bag filled with random topics (see *List of Writing Topics,* page 34)

Overview

Students will identify and recognize significant details in nonfiction text and include significant details in their writing.

Planning

Before the lesson begins, write out a list of random topics, such as locations, television shows or movies, sports or recreation activities, and famous people or events. Write one topic per slip of paper, and place all the slips in a paper bag for students to draw from. The topic they draw will be the topic they write their paragraph about.

Procedure

Modeling

1. Tell students that one of the problems many people have with writing is that they don't know what to say about their topic. In this lesson, students will learn a strategy for adding strong details to their writing.

2. Distribute three colored sticky notes or note cards to each student: one red, one green, and one yellow (or other colors as appropriate).

3. Tell students there are three kinds of key details they can look for when they read. These are *descriptions or definitions, causes and effects,* or *comparisons.*

4. Ask students to explain *description or definition.* Ask students how they know when they are reading a description or a definition. What are some of the key clue words that alert them? Have students write *describe or define* on their red sticky note and add a few of the clue words they brainstormed.

5. To differentiate for language learners, ask students to come up with a hand motion or signal that represents *describe or define.* Practice the signal a few times while saying *describe or define.*

6. Repeat steps 4 and 5 for the term *cause and effect,* using the green sticky note and choosing a different hand motion.

7. Repeat steps 4 and 5 for the term *compare and contrast,* using the yellow sticky note and choosing a different hand motion.

Guided Practice

8. Display a short nonfiction passage on the board and distribute copies to students. Ask students to read the passage silently while you read it aloud. Every time they hear one of the clue words they wrote on their sticky notes, they should hold up that color sticky note.

9. Read a few lines together until you feel students can continue on their own. Have students use additional sticky notes or markers to identify clue words in the text that identify definitions or descriptions, causes and effects, or comparisons.

10. Have a few students share the clues they identified.

11. Tell students that if they were able to recognize these details when they read, they should be able to add these kinds of details to their writing.

12. Model for students, if necessary, using a simple topic, such as cats or roller coasters. Display a large version of the *Main Ideas and Details Activity Sheets,* and demonstrate how you add definitions or descriptions, causes and effects, and comparisons about the topic.

Independent Practice

13. Distribute copies of the *Main Ideas and Details* activity sheet to students. Have each student draw one topic from the paper bag, and ask them to fill in the activity sheet about the topic.

14. Tell students this was a prewriting activity. After they have completed their activity sheets, they should keep the sheets in their Reading and Writing Portfolio to use again in the next lesson.

15. Allow a few students to share their details.

Main Ideas and Details

Name: _____

Main Ideas and Details

Directions: Choose a topic. Use the graphic organizer below to record interesting, significant details about the topic.

Topic:
Define or describe your topic:
Name a cause or effect about your topic:
Compare or contrast your topic with something:

List of Writing Topics

Bubble gum	Sea anemones
Cheetahs	Baseball
World Wrestling Federation	Beach volleyball
Cantaloupe	Heroism
Fear	Yellow
Firefighters	Paris
George Washington	Martin Luther King Jr.
Trampolines	Rollerblading
Science fiction	Poodles
Family	Chocolate ice cream
Vegetarians	Cartoons
Comedies	Gardening

Mini-Lesson: Topic and Concluding Sentences

Common Core State Standard

Introduce a topic clearly, previewing what is to follow; organize ideas, concepts, and information, using strategies such as definition, classification, comparison/contrast, and cause/effect; include formatting (e.g., headings), graphics (e.g., charts, tables), and multimedia when useful to aiding comprehension; provide a concluding statement or section that follows from and supports the information or explanation presented.

Materials

- Reading and Writing Portfolio
- Glue sticks
- Chart paper
- Cardstock cut into sentence strips
- Colored paper
- Scissors
- *Main Ideas and Details* activity sheet (from previous lesson)
- *Topic Sentence Graphic Organizer,* page 37

Overview

Students will assemble a paragraph by organizing their ideas using sentence strips. They will learn various ways to start a paragraph with an interesting topic sentence and then write a parallel sentence as a concluding statement. Students will collect interesting topic and concluding sentences and add them to their Reading and Writing Portfolios.

Planning

Have enough sentence strips available for students to have five to seven each. Cut colored paper into squares that will fit into the Reading and Writing Portfolio.

Procedure

Modeling

1. Have students refer to their *Main Ideas and Details* activity sheets. Review the types of details students used to describe their topics: definitions and descriptions, causes and effects, and comparisons.

2. Distribute copies of the *Topic Sentence Graphic Organizer* to students. Ask students to write the topic from the previous lesson in the center circle.

3. Have students label Box 1 *Sound Effect.* Ask students to help you co-construct a definition of a sound effect and write it on chart paper. Have students brainstorm examples of sound effects and then write the definition in their own words on their graphic organizer. Ask students to write a sentence about their topic that starts with a sound effect.

4. Have students label Box 2 *Adverb.* On chart paper, ask students to help you co-construct a definition of an adverb. Have students brainstorm examples of adverbs and then write the definition in their own words on their graphic organizer. Ask students to write a sentence about their topic that starts with an adverb.

5. Repeat step 3 using the term *Question* for Box 3 and the term *Prepositional Phrase* for Box 4.

Guided Practice

6. Tell students to write each of their detail sentences on a separate sentence strip. Have them choose one of the sentences from their graphic organizer to write on another sentence strip. Ask students to save one sentence strip and set it aside for now.

7. Give students a few minutes to organize their detail sentences by moving their sentences around. Ask students to try various orders until they find the one that they think makes the most sense. Tell them to use the sentence from the graphic organizer as their topic sentence.

8. Ask students to evaluate whether their paragraph makes sense or whether more clarifying information is needed. Clarifying information might offer a deeper explanation or add more details. Clarifying information might also include a picture, a chart, or data. Challenge students to choose at least two ways to add more information by elaborating on what they already wrote. (Note: Students should not be thinking of *new* information to add, but rather information that *elaborates* or *substantiates* what they have already written.)

9. When students are pleased with their paragraph, have them write a concluding sentence that sums up the paragraph. Tell students the concluding sentence must use the same technique as the topic sentence. For example, if the topic sentence started with an adverb, then the concluding sentence should also start with an adverb.

Independent Practice

10. Give students time to write out their paragraph, either by hand or using the computer. Allow students to insert graphics or other elements to elaborate on their details.

11. Have students glue two colored squares into their Reading and Writing Portfolios to serve as pockets. Tell them to label one pocket *Topic Sentences* and the other pocket *Concluding Sentences*.

12. Tell students that as they read nonfiction text, they can collect interesting topic sentences and concluding sentences and write them on index cards to keep in the pockets. These will serve as references for future writing projects.

Topic and Concluding Sentences

Name:_____

Topic Sentence Graphic Organizer

Box 1

Box 2

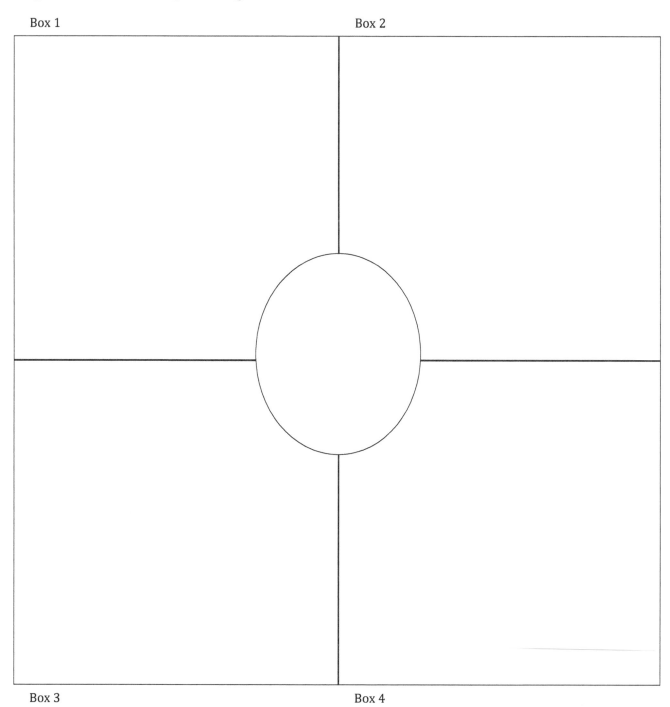

Box 3

Box 4

Chapter 2

Response to Literature

Overview: How to Respond to Text

The anchor standards for writing outlined in the Common Core State Standards describe a set of standards categorized as *Research to Build and Present Knowledge*. This category includes the specific standard "Draw evidence from literary or informational texts to support analysis, reflection, and research."

The implication for students is that they should have a deep comprehension of the text they are reading and that they can pick out the specific details in the text that inform their analysis.

The connection to reading is evident in the expectations. Students must be able to read closely to find the significant details they will use as evidence. Many students and struggling readers, in particular, have trouble understanding exactly what is meant by a *significant detail*. When they read, everything is given equal weight, and distinguishing what is important from what is superfluous can be challenging. The lessons in this section define the types of significant details students should look for according to each text type.

By providing an identifying label, students can read more purposefully because they are looking for very specific clue words that will alert them when a line is important. Once they find it in their reading, they can discuss it with authority in their writing. This type of analysis is excellent practice for writing original works because students will have had exposure on the ways to support a main idea. When it is their turn to write in a specific text type, they can be reminded of mentor texts they have read that have served as models.

Reading Strategy: Responding to Explanatory/Informational Text

Adolescents typically struggle with text analysis. They may be able to identify a line or element that is being used as a specific literary device, but they have trouble understanding why the author made that choice. Learning how to make specific choices as writers themselves will help students see written text from a new perspective.

The continued and prevalent use of high-stakes writing tests demonstrates the need for effective responses to literature. Regardless of genre, students need tools to help them perform close readings under a tight time constraint. They will need tools that will help them discern the significance of elements and then transfer that analysis skill across multiple platforms.

Close reading means that students purposefully examine text. They need practice looking at all the elements of text, from organization and text structure to specific features of text, such as headings, diagrams, photos, and captions. Secondary teachers assume that students have a working knowledge of how their textbooks function and innately understand the purpose of each element. But a social studies book is laid out differently from a mathematics book, and both are different from a novel. Compound the problem by the fact that technology has changed the way adolescents take in information (holistically versus sequentially), and it's easy to see why students have a hard time accessing complex reading materials.

Focus: Supporting Details

Once they identify the text features and understand their functions, students are on their way to understanding the many types of details that authors rely upon to support their ideas. Responding to explanatory and informational text allows students opportunities to evaluate the effectiveness of various types of supporting details, which can lead to their making more informed choices about the kinds of details they use to support their own ideas when they write.

The following Mini-Lesson shows students several types of evidence that are appropriate to supporting a main idea in an explanatory or informational text. Students will define these details and then practice identifying them by using specific clue words. Then, students will demonstrate understanding by writing a statement showing they recognize the type of detail and the purpose it serves.

Mini-Lesson: Text Features and Significant Details

Common Core State Standard

Draw evidence from literary or informational texts to support analysis, reflection, and research.

Materials

- Sample textbooks, cookbooks, reference materials, or websites (one per student)
- *Text Features Graphic Organizer*, page 42
- *Connecting Reading to Writing Chart*, page 43
- *Reading Strategy Game Cards* (several sets for groups of students), page 44
- *Reading Strategy Game Tally Sheet*, page 45

Overview

Students will be introduced to various text features and analyze each feature's purpose. They will also be introduced to six types of significant details that are most often used to support main ideas in explanatory text. Students will complete a graphic organizer to use as a reference for types of text features and significant details.

Planning

Many types of books can be used for this lesson. Have students bring in texts they use from other classes, or print a page of a popular website to use as an example. The texts or pages chosen for display should have several text features represented, such as charts, maps, diagrams, several fonts, headings, photos or illustrations with captions, tables, and so on.

Procedure

Modeling

1. Tell students they will be learning about text features and types of significant details that most commonly appear in informational text. Distribute copies of the *Text Features Graphic Organizer* to students. Give each student one textbook or reference text.

2. Display a sample page from a textbook or use a page from a website. Display the page either through a computer-based projector or a document camera.

3. Post a sheet of chart paper and draw a three-column chart. Label the columns as follows: *Feature, Description, Purpose.* Have students refer to the chart on their graphic organizers.

4. Ask students to call out some of the features they notice within the displayed text. Students should notice fonts, headings, sidebars, photos, diagrams, captions, tables, tabs, and so on. Chart students' answers in the *Feature* column on the chart paper.

5. Choose one feature, such as headings. Ask students to describe a heading. Answers may include: *words that are larger than the paragraph, words in bold, words set off from the rest of a paragraph.* Chart student answers. Have students write the feature and the description on their graphic organizers.

6. Ask students to explain the purpose of a heading. Think aloud to help students understand that a heading can serve as a title, a mini-summary, or a description of the main idea of the text that follows.

Guided Practice

7. Have students work with partners to choose two more features each and add them to their graphic organizers.

8. Have students refer to the *Connecting Reading to Writing* chart. Explain to students that when they read explanatory text, they use specific reading strategies. Point to the left side of the chart, and identify *visualize, predict, connect, question, infer,* and *summarize.*

9. Point to the right side of the chart, and explain how authors help readers use those strategies: by adding *descriptive details* the reader can *visualize,* by adding *causes and effects* the reader can predict what will happen next, by adding *comparisons* the reader can *connect,* by adding *interesting or unusual facts* the reader can *question,* by adding *personal examples* the reader can *infer,* and by using a *specific* structure the reader can *summarize.*

10. Have students read the examples on the chart with a partner. Ask students to discuss and share out loud how the examples are indicative of the author's use of a strategy.

Independent Practice

11. Ask students to work in groups of four. Distribute copies of the *Reading Strategy Game Cards* and *Reading Strategy Game Tally Sheets* to students. Explain that they will take turns pulling a card and deciding which type of reading strategy is represented on the card. Students will rotate playing the role of the judge, who will choose the card, read the description, and wait for classmates to provide the answer. Then, the judge will give the correct answer for that round. After each round, the role of the judge rotates one person to the left. The judge will tally on the tally sheet the number of correct responses for each student.

12. For an extra point, students who get the correct answer can create a new example, and the rest of the students must judge whether it represents the strategy accurately.

13. After the game, have students write an explanation in their own words of each type of detail they examined and its purpose in informational text.

Text Features and Significant Details

Name: _____

Text Features Graphic Organizer

Directions: Fill in the chart below with features you can find in your text. Describe each feature and explain the purpose of that feature in the text

Feature	Description	Purpose
heading	words that are larger than the paragraph; words in bold; words set off by two line spaces	title, a mini-summary, or a description of the main idea of the text that follows

Text Features and Significant Details

Connecting Reading to Writing Chart

For a reader to:	The writer must:
Visualize	**Use descriptive words** **Ex.:** The green, leafy tree grew at a steep angle away from the jagged cliff.
Predict	**Show clear causes and effects** **Ex.:** A 2,000-calorie-per-day diet has been generally approved as reasonable for most people. When more than 2,000 calories are consumed in a day, there are some obvious effects on a person's health and weight.
Make connections	**Make comparisons** **Ex.:** The assembly line allowed the automobile to quickly become an affordable household staple, unlike other luxury items.
Question	**Provide interesting and unusual facts** **Ex.:** Because the comet is rarely seen twice in a lifetime, complicated mathematical calculations were necessary to prove its orbit.
Infer	**Use relatable or personal examples** **Ex.:** Being forced from his home at such an early age, the boy had a strong survival instinct. The rescuers were comforted by that thought.
Summarize	**Organize information logically** **Ex.:** The problem of an energy shortage can be addressed through three important solutions.

Reading Strategy Game Cards

Look for the bus stop sign. It has a red bar under a white box. *Visualize*	A plant cell has a very thick cell wall (a membrane), and a well-defined nucleus. This may look like a dark circular area. *Visualize*	Roads and waterways surrounded Rome and helped the city maintain its strength and authority, but the borders of the whole empire were too vast for the military to effectively handle. *Predict*
Even though slavery had been abolished, so many racist organizations sprang up that many African-Americans migrated north to New York City. *Predict*	The nucleus is like the brain of the plant cell because the nucleus is in charge of everything the cell has to do. *Connect*	To show how a part of something relates to a whole, use a pie chart or circle graph. This is a circle divided into sections, like a pizza. *Connect*
The longest python found was 10 feet but was later measured at 11 feet. Clearly it is difficult to measure a python. *Question*	It is believed that Ra, the Egyptian sun god, created himself from a pyramid-shaped mound of earth. Then he created all other gods. *Question*	Long ago a "land bridge" of Panama connected North and South America. This bridge allowed some species of animals to migrate, which led to diversity even among animals of the same species. *Infer*
Listen to the tone of her voice. If she's shy, the tone of her voice might be a little softer than normal and she might start to play with her hair. *Infer*	Every trip has a beginning and ending, and using the Metro is no different. You must first decide where you will begin, where you want to go, and when you want to travel. *Summarize*	Be sure to pay attention to the title or heading of every visual. These will help you understand the topic, as well as offer information about the type of information you are looking at. *Summarize*

Reading Strategy Game
Tally Sheet

Directions: Write the name of each player in the top row. Keep track of each time that player correctly identifies the reading strategy. Award an extra point if the player can correctly name a similar example. If the player gets the strategy wrong but could make a strong argument for it, players vote on whether to award that player a point.

Reading Strategy: Responding to Argument Text

The writing anchor standards indicate that students should be able to "gather relevant information from multiple print and digital sources" and "assess the credibility and accuracy of each source." To help students be college and career ready for the twenty-first century, the definition of text must be expanded to include online content, billboards, posters, and even packaging designs. Writing is the vehicle that allows students to express the connections between these media. Through writing, students can discuss content in whatever format it may take.

Focus: Types of Appeals

To be critical thinkers, students need practice determining whether information is credible and accurate. Modern writing makes use of multiple persuasive techniques, including visual elements, sound, and music, along with strong word choices and irreverence. Students need to be well versed in identifying each of these elements so they can view the message as a whole with objectivity and with bias at least acknowledged, if not eliminated.

This lesson highlights the various ways that an author can be persuasive and asks students to determine the credibility of that technique in light of the purpose of the text as well as the intended audience. When students can be made aware of these factors, they can read text with a critical eye and be more cognizant of their response. Then students can authoritatively state that they understand why an author chose a particular type of appeal and evaluate the effect of that appeal.

Mini-Lesson: How Appealing!

Common Core State Standard

Gather relevant information from multiple print and digital sources, assess the credibility and accuracy of each source, and integrate the information while avoiding plagiarism.

Materials

- Notebook paper or scrap paper
- Several sample argument texts for display
- Cardstock
- *Appeals Chart,* page 48
- *Appeals Cube* net (one per group), page 49
- *Audience and Purpose Cube* net (one per group), page 50
- *Credibility Measure Worksheet,* page 51

Overview

Students will practice responding to various types of persuasive techniques by judging appeals used for a variety of purposes and with specific audiences in mind.

Planning

The cubes for the game can be made ahead of time by using the nets provided.

Procedure

Modeling

1. Tell students that argument text relies on different types of appeals to prove a point, depending on the purpose of the argument and the audience.
2. Distribute copies of the *Appeals Chart* to students and familiarize them with the definitions of each type of appeal.
3. Display the sample argument text, and model how to identify each type of appeal in the text.

Guided Practice

4. Check for understanding and have students pair-share with a partner and then share with the class the examples they were able to find.
5. Distribute copies of the *Credibility Measure Worksheet.* Model how to fill in the worksheet by entering a sample appeal in the first column. Think aloud as you complete the rating. Ask students whether the appeal is credible.
6. Explain to students that pure logic is usually credible if the purpose of the appeal involves an authority figure or is related to a law or rule. An emotional appeal may be credible if the purpose of the appeal involves someone's feelings or if the audience is young or emotional. Ask students to brainstorm examples of appeals that might be credible for different reasons.

Independent Practice

7. Have students work in groups of three. Give each group one *Appeals Cube* and one *Audience and Purpose Cube.* Explain the game using the worksheet.
8. After the game, ask students to write an explanation in their own words on this topic: What makes an argument credible? Be sure students use the correct academic vocabulary in their description.

Appeals Chart

Emotional Appeals	Logical Appeals
Bandwagon	Testimonial
Name-calling	Black-and-White Fallacy
Repetition	Missing Data
Transfer	Deductive Reasoning
Emotional Words	Factual Evidence

Appeals Cube

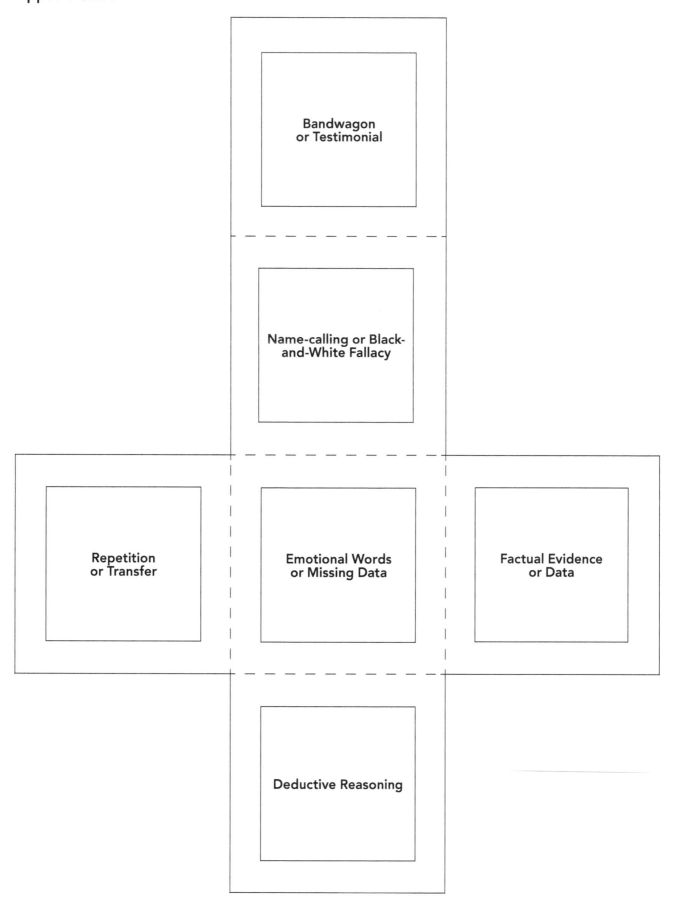

Bandwagon or Testimonial

Name-calling or Black-and-White Fallacy

Repetition or Transfer

Emotional Words or Missing Data

Factual Evidence or Data

Deductive Reasoning

Audience and Purpose Cube

Convince an authority figure to change a rule.

Stand up to a bully and convince him or her to leave you alone.

Persuade someone younger than you to ride a scary roller coaster.

Convince a teacher to be the moderator of a new club.

Write a letter to a newspaper about an injustice you want to fix.

Justify to your parents why you deserve a new privilege.

Credibility Measure Worksheet

Name: _____

Directions: One student is the judge, and that person will roll the cubes. The other two students have two minutes to write an appeal based on what is rolled. After two minutes, students turn their appeals over to the judge, who rates the credibility of each appeal using the rating below. The person whose appeal is most credible wins the round, and the role of the judge rotates to another player. Play ends when each person has had a chance to be judge twice.

Type of Appeal	Rating					Credible?
	Entirely based on emotion	Strongly based on emotion	Some emotion some logic	Strongly based on logic	Entirely based on logic	
						yes maybe no
						yes maybe no
						yes maybe no
						yes maybe no
						yes maybe no
						yes maybe no

Reading Strategy: Responding to Narrative Text

It may seem that responding to narrative text is easy. We seem to relate naturally to a narrative since it represents a story or sequence of events, and we are more practiced in this conversational form. But it is just as important for students to recognize what they are responding to when they encounter a narrative. Are they connecting to the author's situation? To the emotions? To the challenge the author faced? Once students can identify why the text has had an impact on them, they can more easily generalize the theme of the text, which will help them write an effective thesis.

Focus: Language and Word Choice

Although many students don't believe it, authors make very deliberate word choices when they write. Reading a text is like having a one-sided conversation with the author. If the student were face to face with the author, the student would have the benefit of seeing the author's expressions, hearing the intonations in his or her voice, and understanding the subtle body language that conveys emotions and tone. In the one-sided conversation that we have as readers, though, the author understands that the only way to convey emotion and tone is through devices, such as words with specific connotative meanings and language that paints a picture.

This lesson allows students to experiment with various literary techniques to see the emotional impact that each one can have. Then students will realize that as narrative writers, they have many tools at their disposal to add emotional punch to their writing.

Mini-Lesson: Literary Devices

Common Core State Standard

Draw evidence from literary or informational texts to support analysis, reflection, and research.

Materials

- Samples of short narrative texts
- *Literary Devices Chart* (to distribute, plus one to display), page 54
- *Support for a Theme* activity sheet, page 55

Overview

Students will examine the various types of literary devices and see how each device can be used to support a theme. Students will practice a strategy for identifying theme by making connections to their own lives.

Planning

Choose short narrative pieces that students can read quickly with partners. Be sure to enforce the correct use of academic language and terminology, and ask students to respond in complete sentences.

Procedure

Modeling

1. Tell students that a narrative is a story or sequence of events, but it could take the form of a poem, a song, a fictional story, a biography, a diary, or a news story. Explain that the purpose of a narrative is to get the reader to understand some important lesson or idea so that the story can help the reader make choices in his or her own life.

2. Distribute the *Literary Devices Chart* to students. Introduce the terminology in the chart, and use examples from various narratives to demonstrate how each device is used. Check for understanding and have students work with partners to explain their understanding of each device in their own words.

Guided Practice

3. Display a sample of a short narrative text, or distribute copies of text to partners. Have students read the text and use the process steps outlined on the *Literary Devices Chart* to identify various literary devices. Have them use the sentence frame as a model to express their responses.

4. Distribute copies of the *Support for a Theme* activity sheet to students. Use a sample narrative to think aloud as you fill in the chart. Complete the first one for students, and then complete a second example with student partners discussing their answers and sharing out.

Independent Practice

5. Distribute a new narrative text. Have students read the text and use the *Literary Devices Chart* and *Support for a Theme* activity sheets to respond to the various devices.

6. Ask students to write a one-paragraph response to the text in which they identify the theme and explain how at least two literary devices they found support that theme.

Literary Devices Chart

Literary Device	Definition	Purpose	Example
Simile	Compare two things or ideas using *like* or *as*	To highlight shared characteristics and create a connection or allusion	The kitten was as white as snow.
Metaphor	Compare two things or ideas	To highlight shared characteristics and add connotative power	Her eyes were sparkly diamonds.
Hyperbole	An exaggerated description	To add humor, or to underscore a quality of a characteristic	He was so smart, he was probably doing algorithms at age 7.
Personification	Giving human characteristics to an animal or object	To help paint a picture; to add emotional impact	The wind whistled through the trees.

Process steps:

1. Read the passage.

2. Identify the figurative language.

3. Ask yourself: Why did the author choose to use this device? (Use the chart to help you.)

4. Explain your answer using the sentence frame below.

This passage is an example of _____

because _____.

The author used this device to _____

_____.

Support for a Theme

Name:_____

Directions: Read a short narrative, and then fill in the chart below. Determine the moral or lesson of the narrative, and then make a connection to yourself. Next, explain how the narrative is talking about a bigger life lesson or theme.

For the character(s): What was the moral of the story (or lesson learned):	For me (choose one): I have experienced a similar... (or: I could experience a similar...)	The author is trying to show me through this story that...
	...emotion when _____ ...fear when _____ ...triumph when _____ ...accomplishment when _____ ...relationship with _____	
	...emotion when _____ ...fear when _____ ...triumph when _____ ...accomplishment when _____ ...relationship with _____	

Chapter 3

Explanatory and Informational Text

Overview of the Genre

Purpose

Explanatory and informational text does just what the text type says: It explains something. In the last chapter, students were introduced to this text type and discovered that there are three main purposes for writing in this style:

- To explain *how* something works (a process)
- To explain *why* something works (a cause and effect)
- To explain a *relationship* (a comparison)

Each type of explanatory text shares similar components, which will help students recognize this kind of writing when they read and also help them include these components as writers. The common elements are what will help strengthen the reading and writing connection.

Audience

Understanding the audience helps students make informed choices about the structure and language to use when they write. A story written for a five year old will use different language and a simpler structure than an essay written for a college professor. Ask students who is usually reading how-to papers. What kind of person would want to know the cause and effect of something? And who might be concerned with comparing two things? When students have a better understanding of who the intended audience is, they can be reading consumers—deciding whether the text they read was written to appeal to them and, if not, why not? Who might it have been written for, and how do they know?

In order to understand intended audience, it will be important for students to have reading put into a context, either historically or topically, in order to make it relevant. Pre-teach any important historical facts and scientific or mathematical principles that are necessary to achieve a true understanding of the text.

Reading Strategy: Predicting

Focus: Text Structure

The first thing students must recognize is the structure of an explanatory text. The strong organizational style of explanatory text will help students as they read because they can better predict what will come next and how to find main ideas and details when they understand the consistent structure. One structure is step by step, which outlines in sequential order a procedure or task. A problem-solution structure presents a description of a problem and then outlines one or more possible solutions. A compare-and-contrast structure will describe one facet or situation first, describe the contrasting facet or situation next, and may end with a paragraph that sums up; or the first paragraph may offer all the ways two things are similar, and the next paragraph might demonstrate all the ways they are different.

Focus: Transition Words

Being able to recognize transition words will help students determine or predict which type of explanatory text they are reading. Typically a process paper will use sequential transitions, such as *first, next, then,* and *finally,* since it is describing a step-by-step procedure. A cause-and-effect text will use transitions, such as *when, then, as a result,* and *after.* A comparison text will use transitions that show similarities and differences, such as *similar to, as opposed to, however,* and *just like.* When students recognize the structure of text and the transition words, they can more easily identify that they are reading an explanatory text, and by determining which type of explanatory text they are reading, they can make a prediction about what will follow.

When students write, they can target key structures and transition words to match their topic. Because they have practiced finding these words in reading and recognizing the specific uses for each type of structure and transition word, they can narrow down their word choices to align to the type of text they are composing.

Reading Strategy: Visualizing

Focus: Descriptive and Sensory Words

One comprehension strategy we ask students to use is visualizing. We want them picturing what they read and creating mental images. This helps students hold on to the words because they can "see" what is happening. To be able to visualize, students need to find those places in the text that are particularly descriptive. Have them look specifically for sensory words. These will anchor their ability to visualize what they are reading. The more senses involved, the stronger the picture will be.

As writers, then, students need to practice adding strong sensory details. They should be as vivid as they can when describing how something looks, feels, tastes, smells, and so on. The more vivid they can be in their descriptions, the better their reader will understand what they're trying to say.

Sometimes the words will not be enough, and the text may include a graphic—a picture, an illustration, or a chart—to serve as additional detail to help explain. Students should be reminded that these visual elements are not included just to take up space. Sometimes the picture or chart is more descriptive than any words could be.

Focus: Word Choice

In addition to creating sensory descriptions, authors choose very specific terms because of the many shades of meaning associated with them. The sentence "The table was made of wood" is not nearly as descriptive as "The dining table was made of caramel-colored chestnut." The second sentence clarifies what kind of table, as well as what kind of wood, and then describes the color of the wood to add even more dimension to the description. The second sentence is definitely easier to picture than the first.

As writers, students need to practice revising their work to look for places where they were vague or ambiguous and tighten up their writing by adding specific adjectives, explicit nouns, and more interesting verbs that will deepen the reader's awareness and understanding of the topic.

Prerequisite Skills

Because this unit will focus on the reading strategies of summarizing, using text structures, and visualizing, students will need practice with these tools. Provide Mini-Lessons on adjectives, explicit nouns, and active verbs, so students have a store of words from which to choose when it comes time for them to do their own writing. Expose students to texts that utilize different text structures, and have students practice identifying transition words. Use summarizing strategies repeatedly, and have students practice them with short pieces of text as well as long pieces.

Specific Content-area Vocabulary

If students will be writing in a specific content area, front-load the vocabulary they will need so they are familiar with it and can use it comfortably. There are a number of strategies for introducing and practicing vocabulary and for creating and maintaining a word-conscious environment in your classroom. Create word walls, give points or rewards each time students use a vocabulary word in natural conversation, or encourage them to use Frayer maps or other concept-mapping tools so they make strong connections to words.

During reading, students may still encounter unknown words, so it is important to teach them decoding strategies as well. Some decoding strategies they can use during reading include:

- Look at the context to determine what the word probably means.
- See if the word is defined in the text by an example or a non-example.
- Look at the root words and try to cipher out the meaning.
- Determine the part of speech to help understand how the word is being used.

Sample Planning Calendar

Decide on a culminating assignment (some ideas are provided across content areas at the end of this section on page 82). Enter the due date for this project at the end of the third week or the beginning of the fourth week of instruction. Work backward to introduce reading and writing instruction and guided practice opportunities. Allow time for comprehension checks, Mini-Lessons, re-teaching, and test prep. A sample of a four-week unit on explanatory/informational writing appears below.

Monday	Tuesday	Wednesday	Thursday	Friday
RI: Visualization	RP: Visualization	WI: Observations	WP: Observations	RP/WP: Visualization Observations
RI: Text Structures	RI: Predicting	RP: Text Structures WI: Processes	RP: Predicting WP: Processes	RP: Text Structures V: Transitional Words
RI: Main Ideas and Details	RP: Main Ideas and Details WI: Supporting Details	WP: Supporting Details WI: Openings and Closings	RI: Word Choice WI: Sentence Structure G: Adverbs, Gerunds, Prepositional Phrases	WP: Drafting Culminating Project (optional placement)
WP: Revising Culminating Project (optional placement)	RP: Comprehension Check	WP: Editing G: Adverbs, Gerunds, Prepositional Phrases TEST PREP	TEST PREP	TEST PREP

Legend

RI = Reading Instruction
RP = Reading Practice
WI = Writing Instruction
WP = Writing Practice
V   = Vocabulary
G   = Grammar

Writing Strategy Overview: Sensory and Descriptive Writing

For many students, the idea of writing feels like torture. They think of writing as a magical gift that was bestowed upon some lucky students but not upon them. These students never hear a voice in their head when they read, and they can't think of how to put into words all the things they want to say.

These students need to see that writing is indeed a process and that when they break it down into tiny steps, it becomes more manageable and less scary. Instead of focusing on *everything* they want to say, start small by focusing on one thing at a time. And above all else, make writing experiential, so that students have a real-life experience to hang on to. This will enhance their descriptions and their writing.

For this strategy, students will practice sensory and descriptive writing by making observations using all their senses. They will also describe a process using as many descriptive terms as they can to be explicit and detailed. Through guided prewriting activities, students will see how they can add rich dimension to their words and expand their writing even further.

Use these lessons during the prewriting stage of the writing process to get students in a frame of mind for writing and to fill their word banks with rich and varied word choices.

Prewriting Mini-Lesson: Observations

Common Core State Standard

Develop the topic with relevant facts, definitions, concrete details, quotations, or other information and examples.

Materials

- Beach ball
- Chart paper
- Resealable plastic bags
- Lemons, oranges, or some other fruit cut in half and placed in the plastic bags
- Reading and Writing Portfolio
- *Text Types and Purposes Reference Sheet,* page 20
- *Observation* activity sheet, page 63

Overview

Students will practice using sensory details to describe a piece of fruit.

Planning

Before the lesson begins, cut the fruit in half and place half pieces in each plastic bag. This lesson can be used as part of a culminating assignment in which students make repeated observations and then write an explanatory essay about the decomposition of the fruit. See the "Culminating Project Ideas" on page 82 for additional assignments.

Procedure

Modeling

1. Hold up an inflatable beach ball. Ask students what it is.
2. Label one sheet of chart paper *See.* Ask students to describe what they see. Write down all of their ideas, including colors, shapes, size, and so on.
3. Label another sheet of chart paper *Feel.* Have a few students touch the beach ball and describe how it feels. Give them some words to help, such as *smooth, slick, rubbery,* and *bouncy.*
4. Ask students to tell you some other ways they could describe the ball (possible responses include *how it sounds, smells, moves*).

Guided Practice

5. Ask students to work in groups of four. Distribute copies of the *Observation* activity sheets to students.
6. Give each group one plastic bag with fruit. Tell students they may open the bag to smell the fruit or they may reach in one finger to touch it, but they may not take the fruit out of the bag or spill the juice out of the bag.
7. On their activity sheet, have students work together to describe the fruit. They should write at least three things for each category: how it looks, how it smells, how it feels, its shape, its size, whether anything else is happening to the fruit in the bag.

Independent Practice

8. Have students share their descriptions. Keep track of words that are used frequently, such as *yellow* or *smooth*.

9. Have students look at their lists and circle those frequently-used words. Challenge students to use a thesaurus to find different words to substitute for those common words.

10. Take digital photos of the fruit and have students write a paragraph about their photo, either on paper or on a computer, using unique words they could find. Or have students write riddles about their piece of fruit using their descriptions as clues.

11. Put the bags away and take them out for a few days for students to make a second and third observation, noticing how things have changed, and comparing the changes with their descriptions.

Reading Connection

Give students sticky notes or a bookmark with a symbol on it that represents visualizing. Give students a piece of text, and have them place a sticky note or symbol each time they visualized what they read. Model this for students using a piece of descriptive writing.

Next, have students go back to the places they marked in the text, and ask them to circle or highlight the exact word or words that helped them form a picture in their mind. Ask students to determine how many of those were sensory words. Have them sort the sensory words by sight, touch, smell, sound, or taste. Students can keep a dictionary of sensory words in their Reading and Writing Portfolios and add to their list as they continue reading.

Formative Assessment

If the student...	Consider practicing these prerequisite skills:
had trouble thinking of sensory words	synonyms
had trouble identifying sensory or descriptive words	the five senses; metaphors and similes

Prewriting Mini-Lesson

Name:_____

Observation

Directions: Write down what you observe in the chart below.

Characteristic	Day 1	Day 2	Day 3
Color			
Texture			
Size			
Shape			
Smell			
In the Bag			
Other			

Prewriting Mini-Lesson: Processes

Common Core State Standard

Use precise language and domain-specific vocabulary to inform about or explain the topic.

Materials

- Reading and Writing Portfolio
- Unusual objects, such as an apple corer or a miter box (without saw)
- *Text Types and Purposes Reference Sheet,* page 20
- *Be Specific!* activity sheet, page 66
- *Precise or Not Precise? Topic Cards,* page 67

Overview

Students will replace general terms with more explicit and precise terminology.

Planning

Show students a clip from the television show "The Amazing Race." Ask students what makes the tasks so difficult for the contestants. (The contestants don't have the skills or understanding to complete the tasks easily.) Tell students that when writing descriptively, they must make their descriptions as clear and easy to follow as possible.

Procedure

Modeling

1. Hold up an object or a picture of an object, such as an apple corer, or a tool, such as a miter box, that is unusual and probably unfamiliar to students. Ask students whether they have seen or used anything like this before.
2. Ask student volunteers to come up and describe the item for the class and explain how to use it.
3. Give students the specific names of the parts of the object. Ask another volunteer to explain how to use it, using the specific terminology.
4. Ask students which description was clearer.
5. Tell students that when writing descriptively, the more precise they can be in their terminology, the clearer their descriptions will be.

Guided Practice

6. Ask students to work with partners. Distribute copies of the *Be Specific!* activity sheet to students.
7. Give each pair of students a set of *Precise or Not Precise? Topic Cards.* Have them turn over one card at a time and determine the following: Is the topic precise or not precise? If it is precise, have them add the term that makes it precise to their activity sheets. If it is not precise, have them brainstorm a more specific term and then add that term to their activity sheets.
8. Have students share some of the terms they created, as well as some they identified as precise.

9. Ask students to choose an object or an item from home and describe what it is and how it is used.

10. Have students include a picture or diagram of the object, with all the parts labeled with their exact name.

Reading Connection

As students are reading, have them cross out any terms that are too general and replace them with more specific language. If they come across specific and precise descriptions, have them circle those terms and add them to their "Descriptive Language" pocket in their Reading and Writing Portfolios.

Formative Assessment

If the student...	Consider practicing this prerequisite skill:
had trouble thinking of precise terminology	proper nouns and adjectives

Prewriting Mini-Lesson

Name:_____

Be Specific!

Directions: Use the *Precise or Not Precise? Topic Cards.* Write the topic in the first column of the chart below, and determine whether the topic is precise or general. Indicate your choice in the chart below. Write the specific term that aided you in your decision in the third column.

Topic	Precise?		Specific Term or Replacement
	Yes	No	

Car	Tree	Dog	Cat
Fedora	Red	Skate	Flower
Bug	Tarantula	Movie star	George Clooney
Comedy	Princess	Jacket	Playing card

Writing Strategy Overview: Transitions

The key to strong organization in writing is in the transitions. Starting a paragraph with a strong opening sentence, and finishing it with a final thought encapsulates each main idea and compartmentalizes those ideas in meaningful chunks that are accessible to the reader. The reader has time to process and understand each specific main idea before moving on to the next idea. Writing this way keeps the reader—and the writer—on track and helps minimize tangents that can lead them both astray.

Just as a paragraph deserves a strong structure with a clear beginning and ending, the entire body of the text also needs a strong structure, with a clear opening and a solid ending. An opening paragraph should snatch the reader out of his or her daily life and focus all his or her attention on the reading he or she is about to encounter. To do that requires that the writer consider the context within which this piece is being written and set up that context so that the reader can easily follow. There are a number of ways that the writer can do this, and each way is effective for different reasons. When a student understands some of the options for starting a piece of writing and how to align the option to the purpose and audience for which he or she is writing, the writing becomes clearer, stronger, and more purposeful.

From the reader's perspective, following the writer's thought process should be enjoyable and straightforward. The reader should have a clear sense of the direction that the writing is taking, and to that end, should clearly know when the journey is over. That is why a strong conclusion is so important. Have you ever absentmindedly eaten a bag of potato chips or chocolate chip cookies, maybe while watching television? You've been reaching in the bag over and over, and all of a sudden the bag is empty. How do you feel? Chances are, you feel frustrated that you didn't know you were almost out because had you known, you would have consciously savored that last chip or that final cookie. The reader who is enjoying a piece of text wants to know that the end is coming so that he or she can savor every word and experience a satisfying sense of closure.

The following lessons can be used during the drafting stage of the writing process, when the student has organized his or her thoughts and is ready to finish the text with a strong opening and a substantial closing.

Drafting Mini-Lesson: Openings

Common Core State Standard

Introduce a topic clearly, previewing what is to follow.

Materials

- Reading and Writing Portfolio
- *Text Types and Purposes Reference Sheet,* page 20
- Paragraphs from the "Main Ideas and Details" lesson (pages 35–36)
- *Explanatory Openings* activity sheet, page 71

Overview

Students will learn various options for creating strong opening paragraphs.

Planning

Read the book *Zoom!* by Istvan Banyai (Viking, 1995) as a way to introduce zooming in from a general or broad idea to a specific one. Students should have access to the paragraphs they wrote for the "Main Ideas and Details" activity.

Procedure

Modeling

1. Have students refer to their *Text Types and Purposes Reference Sheet.* Review the purpose of explanatory writing (to explain), argument (to persuade), and narrative (to tell a story or relate a series of events).

2. Show students the book *Zoom!* by Istvan Banyai. After students have seen all the pages, ask them what the big picture was. How does knowing the big picture influence their ideas about the smaller details?

3. Write a list of grocery items on the board: *spaghetti, yogurt, dog food, soap, oatmeal.* Ask students where each of these items would be found in the grocery store (pasta aisle, dairy section, pet aisle, cleaning aisle, cereal aisle). Explain to students that we categorize items so they have logical places and because the big picture of the categories is easier to remember than all the small details.

4. Tell students that writing needs to give the audience a sense of the big picture, so that the reader has a context within which to understand the text. The opening paragraph of any paper provides that big picture by outlining the main points that will be addressed. That way the reader knows what to expect and looks forward to what he or she will find.

5. Tell students that if the purpose of a text is to explain something, the writer should appeal to the reader by giving a relevant reason for knowing this information. Tell students they will learn two ways to start a paper. The first is with three questions, and the second is with a shocking statistic.

6. Write the word *spaghetti* on the board. Tell students to pretend that this is their topic. Within what context would they find spaghetti? Students should say *pasta* or *Italian food.*

7. Ask students for three other types of pasta or Italian food. Write their suggestions above the word *spaghetti* on the board (for example, *lasagna, macaroni,* and *penne*).

8. Have students brainstorm a question about each type of pasta. (e.g., *Have you ever tried lasagna? What is so great about macaroni and cheese? Why does penne look like tubes?*)

9. Tell students these questions are the "hook" for the text and provide a context for their topic: spaghetti. Their next sentence should introduce the topic: *Spaghetti is probably what most people think of when they think of pasta.*

10. After the hook and the topic have been introduced, students should lay out the road map for their readers by listing the main ideas about their topic that will be addressed. In our example, the writer might say, *Spaghetti has been around for centuries, but it wasn't invented in Italy. It actually came from China! Today spaghetti is one of the world's most popular meals.*

11. This format (hook, topic, main ideas) will set up the writing.

12. Another option instead of three questions is to start with a shocking statistic. (Note: The statistic doesn't have to be true for this example. Later, students can use real statistics that they find through research.) Substitute a surprising statistic for the three questions in the example above: *Ninety-eight countries around the world eat some form of pasta. Spaghetti is probably what most people think of when they think of pasta. Spaghetti has been around for centuries.*

Guided Practice

13. Distribute copies of the *Explanatory Openings* activity sheet to students.

14. Have students use the topics they wrote about from the "Main Idea and Details" Mini-Lesson. Students will use this topic to fill out the hook and topic portions of their *Explanatory Openings* activity sheet.

15. Assist students as necessary as they think of their own three questions and surprising statistics.

Independent Practice

16. Challenge students to add three main ideas to their *Explanatory Openings* activity sheet based on the details they added to their original paragraphs.

17. Have students save these activity sheets in their Reading and Writing Portfolios as models of how to write opening paragraphs for explanatory writing.

Reading Connection

While students are reading, have them identify the characteristics of opening paragraphs that hook them into the text. Have them keep examples of strong openings in an "Openings" pocket in their Reading and Writing Portfolio.

Formative Assessment

If the student...	Consider practicing these prerequisite skills:
had trouble thinking of three questions	using the 5 Ws
had trouble thinking of main ideas	significant details

Drafting Mini-Lesson

Name:_____

Explanatory Openings

Surprising Statistic or Three Questions:

```



```

Topic:

```

```

Main Ideas:

```




```

Drafting Mini-Lesson: Closings

Common Core State Standard

Provide a concluding statement or section that follows from and supports the information or explanation presented.

Materials

- Reading and Writing Portfolio
- *Text Types and Purposes Reference Sheet,* page 20
- Paragraphs from the "Main Ideas and Details" lesson (pages 35–36)
- *Explanatory Openings* activity sheet from previous lesson
- *Explanatory Closings* activity sheet, page 74

Overview

Students will create parallel structures by using a technique in their closing paragraph similar to what they used in their opening.

Planning

Create a version of the *Explanatory Openings* and *Explanatory Closings* activity sheets that can be used for display on an interactive whiteboard or with a document camera or overhead projector.

Procedure

Modeling

1. Have students refer to their *Explanatory Openings* activity sheets. Display the *Explanatory Openings* and *Explanatory Closings* sheets side by side for students. The *Explanatory Openings* should be filled in from the previous lesson.

2. Tell students they may have heard writing compared to a hamburger. This comparison simply shows that the opening and closing should consist of the same things and that the meat of the essay is in the middle. The opening and closing are different from the middle, but they are necessary to support everything that's in the heart of the paper.

3. If a statistic was used, point to the surprising statistic in the opening paragraph. Tell students that if a surprising statistic is offered to start, then another statistic should be offered in the closing. This statistic should offer similar information but be a different statistic. For example, if the opening paragraph began with *Ninety-eight countries around the world eat some form of pasta,* then the closing paragraph could begin with *Pasta is a main dish in the unlikeliest of countries, including China, Sri Lanka, and India.*

4. If students used the three-questions technique to open their paragraph, then the closing paragraph should begin by answering or responding to those questions. The purpose of this is to bring the reader full circle and to encapsulate all the ideas in a cohesive structure. For example, if the opening paragraph began with, *Have you ever tried lasagna? What is so great about macaroni and cheese? Why does penne look like tubes?*, then the closing paragraph could begin with *Lasagna is a dish with baked pasta that is meaty and delicious. Macaroni and cheese makes lunch enjoyable in school cafeterias everywhere. Tube-shaped pasta like penne is just one way that pasta can be made in creative shapes and sizes.*

5. Next, show students how to restate their topic.

6. Then, show students how to pull a supporting detail from their paragraph and use it in place of restating the main idea. This will serve as a reminder to the reader of the text.

7. Finally, have students write "the last word." This should be a line that expresses what they have learned, what they now understand, or what they want the reader to understand.

Guided Practice

8. Distribute the *Explanatory Closings* activity sheet and have students fill in the spaces.

Independent Practice

9. Instruct students to use their paragraph, their openings, and their closings to write a cohesive paragraph.

Reading Connection

As students are reading, have them identify the characteristics of closing paragraphs that finalize what they read. Have them keep examples of strong closings in a "Closings" pocket in their Reading and Writing Portfolio.

Formative Assessment

If the student...	Consider practicing this prerequisite skill:
had trouble answering the three questions	sentence structures

Drafting Mini-Lesson

Name:_____

Explanatory Closings

Restate the Surprising Statistic or Answer/Respond to the Three Questions:

Restate Topic::

Offer Details about the Main Ideas:

Writing Strategy Overview: Choose the Right Word

Students often think that once they have completed their draft, their work is over. To a large extent, it is. The hardest part of the writing—turning raw ideas into an organized piece of text—is difficult. But the work is not over yet.

The revision process requires a bit of trust on the part of the writer. It is difficult to have your hard work critiqued. But students need to recognize that a little distance helps them improve on their work to make it even better, and it is not in any way an indication that they didn't complete their draft correctly or that they forgot something. The purpose of communicating through writing is to get your point across. If your reader missed your point, then you must find another way, a more effective way, to make your point. Getting another opinion helps focus that feedback and provides concrete ways for students to make the small adjustments necessary.

Many students are used to being coached in sports. When the coach gives tips about how to improve a baseball swing or a more effective way to plant your feet before making a free throw in basketball, it is not a criticism of the player's talent. It is merely a helpful tip from an objective observer who knows just what to look for.

Help students feel comfortable with the revision process by including them in co-constructing the review criteria. Use the objectives of the prewriting and drafting Mini-Lessons as your guide, and ask students what a finished paper should include. Use their suggestions, and build a rubric they all feel is attainable. Then, have students review each other's work, looking for very specific criteria outlined on the rubric. This is not a time for students to offer personal opinions. They either see evidence of the objectives or they don't. That will provide each student author with a concise guide as to what still needs to be done on the paper before it is ready for publishing.

Revising Mini-Lesson: Transitional Word Choices

Common Core State Standard

Determine the meaning of words and phrases as they are used in a text, including figurative and connotative meanings; analyze the impact of specific word choices on meaning and tone, including analogies or allusions to other texts.

Materials

- Chart paper
- Large paper clips
- Index cards
- Timer
- Pictures or wordless video clips that show a sequence of events
- Plastic, sealable bags or wooden blocks (optional)
- *Transition Chains* activity sheet, page 78

Overview

Students will brainstorm transition words and build a reference document to use later for the culminating project. Students will learn about different kinds of transition words and when it is appropriate to use each kind.

Planning

Prepare copies of several pictures that require an explanation of what came before and what may come after, such as a tornado, a child sliding into home plate, and a person who is making a sandwich. (Or, use a wordless video clip.) Place the pictures in plastic sealable bags, or attach them to wooden blocks for durability. Have enough pictures for students to work with partners.

Modeling

1. Display a set of pictures or a short video clip and ask students to describe what they saw. Write student responses (out of order) on a sheet of chart paper displayed in front of the room.
2. Ask students to help you number what happened first, next, and so on to put all the events in order of what happened.
3. Ask students how they knew the order in which to place the sentences. Ask them how they could communicate that idea about order and sequence to their audience.
4. Brainstorm a list of transition words, and have students use them to complete the next steps.

Guided Practice

5. Have students work with partners, and distribute one set of pictures for each pair of students. Ask students to examine the pictures closely and discuss what they think is happening.
6. Tell students they will have two minutes to determine in which order to put the pictures. Set the timer and let students work together to order the events. (Some pairs will have the same set of events but may choose a different order. Students can share their reasons during the discussion.)

7. Once the timer stops, ask several pairs of students to tell the story of their pictures. On a sheet of chart paper, write down each time a student uses a transition word (*first, then, next, after*). Label the chart *Transition Words* and tell students these are words that help move a story along.

8. Ask a few students to try to tell their story without using transition words. Have students share why transition words are important. Write their ideas on the chart.

9. Distribute several large paper clips and a set of eight to 10 index cards to each pair of students. Tell students they will try to think of as many transition words as they can to link their story together. They will write one word on each card. (Encourage students to think of unique words by making this activity a competition, and time students as they try to think of words. Partners who think of the most unique words win the round.)

10. Have students place their cards between or in front of the appropriate places in the story pictures. If more than one card can fit in each spot, have students poke a hole at the bottom of one card and another hole at the top of the second card and then link the cards with the paper clip to form a chain.

11. Ask students to share their words. Display their chains around the room, or link them by categories (e.g., connective words, introduction words, concluding words).

Independent Practice

12. Distribute copies of the *Transition Chains* activity sheet, and have students fill in the word bank with words they used during the lesson. Then, have students write a story, using the events in the pictures and as many of the transition words as they can.

13. Keep index cards and paper clips available, and encourage students to add words to the chains. Students should store their *Transition Chains* activity sheet in their Reading and Writing Portfolios in the "References" pocket.

Reading Connection

As students read, have them identify the transition words they find and write them on individual cards. Have students keep the cards in the "Transition Words" pockets in their Reading and Writing Portfolios.

Formative Assessment

If the student...	Consider practicing this prerequisite skill:
had trouble thinking of transition words	conjunctions

Writing Mini-Lesson

Name: _____

Transition Chains

Directions: Fill in the word bank below with as many transition words as you can. You can add to this word bank as you learn more words.

(empty box)

Use some of the words above to help tell what is happening in the pictures that your teacher showed you.

_____

_____

_____

_____

_____

_____

_____

_____

_____

_____

_____

_____

Revising Mini-Lesson: Sentence Structure

Common Core State Standard

Determine the meaning of words and phrases as they are used in a text, including figurative and connotative meanings; analyze the impact of specific word choices on meaning and tone, including analogies or allusions to other texts.

Materials

- Colored construction paper cut into sets of 3" x 3" cards (one color per set); label each set on one side with a grammatical term: *verb, adjective, noun, adverb, question, exclamation*
- Note cards with simple sentences (one set for each group of students)
- Timer
- *Build a Better Sentence* activity sheet, page 81

Overview

Students will practice using a variety of sentence structures by playing a game in which they turn simple sentences into complex sentences, determined by the colored card chosen.

Preparation

Be sure that students have been introduced to grammatical terms, such as *verbs, adjectives, nouns, adverbs, questions,* and *exclamations.* Create simple sentences on note cards: *Juan runs. Keisha eats. Bobby wakes up. Mom works. Dad drives. Dogs bark. A tree grows. Sand is wet.* (You can laminate the cards for durability.)

Procedure

Modeling

1. Distribute copies of the *Build a Better Sentence* activity sheet to students. Discuss the terms and have students write a definition for each term in the middle column on their activity sheets.

Guided Practice

2. Assign students to work in groups. Tell each student to hold on to his or her activity sheet, and then give each group one set of colored cards (a different color and term per group).

3. Tell students to refer to their activity sheets to remember the definition of the term on their cards. Then have students work together to brainstorm as many examples of the term as they can. Have students write examples on the back of each of the colored cards. (A group with the term *verb* might brainstorm words, such as *run, walk, hop,* or *sleep*; a group with the term *sound effect* might brainstorm words, such as *drip, crash,* or *bang.*) Use a timer and encourage students to think of as many examples as they can in five to 10 minutes. (Students may repeat words.)

4. Once all the groups have added examples to the backs of all their cards, redistribute the groups so that each new group is made up of one member from each of the previous groups.

5. Shuffle the cards and separate them into sets that contain several cards of each color. Give each new group a set of multicolored cards.

6. Distribute a set of *Simple Sentence Cards* to each group of students. Tell students that to play the game, they will take turns drawing one *Simple Sentence Card* and one colored card. Students must restate the simple sentence so that it starts with the term described on the colored card. Students may refer to the example on the back to help them or to the definitions on their activity sheets. For example, if the *Simple Sentence Card* says *Juan runs,* and the colored card is an exclamation card, the student may say, *Wow! Juan runs fast!* (Note: In starting the sentence with a different grammatical term, students may find that they need to alter the structure of the simple sentence or add words to it in order for it to make sense. This encourages students to stretch their thinking and try out more complex sentences.)

Independent Practice

7. Allow students to play enough rounds so that they have had turns trying several types of grammatical terms.

8. Have students return to their own seats. Ask them to write an example sentence for each type of grammar term in the last column on their activity sheets.

9. After you review the activity sheets, ask students to keep these sheets in their Reading and Writing Portfolios in the "References" pocket.

Reading Connection

While students read, have them identify sentence structures and keep them as models. Assign students specific types of structures to look for when they read, such as independent clauses. If students can't find enough variety in their texts, have them choose three to five simple sentences and rewrite them in a more interesting way. Then students examine how each sentences was rewritten and identify the grammatical feature that was changed or added to make the sentence more complex.

Formative Assessment

If the student...	Consider practicing these prerequisite skills:
did not understand one or more of the terms	direct instruction in verbs, nouns, and adjectives
did not change or add to the structure of the simple sentence	simple, complex, and compound sentences

Writing Mini-Lesson

Name:_____

Build a Better Sentence

Directions: In the middle column of the chart below, write a definition for each term listed. In the last column, write a sample sentence that uses that grammatical element as the first word or words.

Term	Definition	Sample Sentence
Adjective		
Adverb		
Noun		
Verb		
Question		
Exclamation		
Sound effect		
Prepositional phrase		

Culminating Project Ideas

Language Arts

Write a travel guide about a unique location, including step-by-step directions and descriptions of events or people at each stop.

Suggested mentor text: *Travels with Charley: In Search of America* by John Steinbeck

Social Studies

Write and film a documentary about a historical figure or event, using appropriate costumes and settings.

Suggested mentor text: *Freedom Walkers: The Story of the Montgomery Bus Boycott* by Russell Freedman

Mathematics

Create a manual for how to build a specific three-dimensional structure. Include descriptions of the individual shapes involved in the building of the structure, and discuss the reasons for each structural choice.

Suggested mentor text: *Cathedral: The Story of Its Construction* by David Macaulay

Science

Describe the decomposition process of a piece of fruit by observing how it changes over a period of several days.

Suggested mentor text: *Invasive Plant Inventory* by California Invasive Plant Council

Additional Resources

Essay Frames

Structure of a body paragraph:
I. Topic sentence: tells main idea
a. Describe
b. Compare
c. Cause/Effect
II. Closing sentence: mirrors main idea

Body Paragraph #1: What is the first idea you want to talk about?

_____

I. Write a topic sentence that addresses this idea. Start with a **verb**.

_____

a. Look back at your observation notes. Use **transition words** and **sensory words** to describe this idea.

_____

_____

_____

_____

b. Make a **comparison**. (Write your answer as a complete sentence.)

_____

_____

_____

c. What do you think was the **cause or effect**? (Write your answer as a complete sentence.)

_____

_____

_____

II. Think of a **verb** that is synonymous with the verb you used above. Write a **closing sentence** using that verb.

_____

_____

_____

HOMEWORK: USE THIS WORKSHEET TO WRITE BODY PARAGRAPH #1, DUE TOMORROW!

> **Structure of a body paragraph:**
>   I. Topic sentence: tells main idea
>   a. Describe
>   b. Compare
>   c. Cause/Effect
>   II. Closing sentence: mirrors main idea

Body Paragraph #2: What is the second idea you want to talk about?

_____

I. Write a topic sentence that addresses this idea. Start with a **clause**.

_____

a. Look back at your observation notes. Use <u>different</u> **transition words,** and <u>new</u> **sensory words** to describe this idea.

_____

_____

_____

_____

b. Make a **comparison**. (Write your answer as a complete sentence.)

_____

_____

_____

c. What do you think was the **cause or effect**? (Write your answer as a complete sentence, but <u>do not use the words</u> *cause* or *effect*.)

_____

_____

_____

II. Think of a **clause** that is synonymous with the clause you used above. Write a **closing sentence** using that clause.

_____

_____

_____

HOMEWORK: USE THIS WORKSHEET TO WRITE BODY PARAGRAPH #2, DUE TOMORROW!

> **Structure of a body paragraph:**
> I. Topic sentence: tells main idea
> a. Describe
> b. Compare
> c. Cause/Effect
> II. Closing sentence: mirrors main idea

Body Paragraph #3: What is the last idea you want to talk about?

_____

I. Write a topic sentence that addresses this idea. Start with a **preposition**.

_____

a. Look back at your observation notes. Use <u>different</u> **transition words,** and <u>new</u> **sensory words** to describe this idea.

_____

_____

_____

_____

b. Make a **comparison**. (Write your answer as a complete sentence.)

_____

_____

_____

c. Give a possible **cause or effect** (Write your answer as a complete sentence, but <u>do not use the words *cause* or *effect*.</u>)

_____

_____

_____

II. Use another **preposition**, and write a **closing sentence** that sums up the paragraph.

_____

_____

_____

HOMEWORK: USE THIS WORKSHEET TO WRITE BODY PARAGRAPH #3,
DUE TOMORROW!

Rubric: Point-based

Format – 20 points

Five paragraphs (introduction, three body paragraphs, conclusion)	5
Typed or handwritten in ink	5
Proper paragraphs	5
Spelling/punctuation	5

Writing Process/Materials – 80 points

Observation journals	20
Three-paragraph worksheets	15
Three-paragraph rough drafts	15
Opening/closing paragraph worksheet	10
Opening/closing paragraph rough draft	10
Peer edit/self-edit	10

Opening Paragraph – 20 points

Title (matches clincher)	5
Three grabber questions	6
Topic	3
Thesis	3
Main ideas	3

Body Paragraph #1 – 20 points

Topic sentence	3
Topic sentence starts with a verb	1
Topic sentence addresses first main idea	1
Describe using sensory descriptions	3
Make a comparison	3
Explain a cause/effect	3
Use three different transition words	3
Closing sentence	2
Closing sentence uses synonymous verb	1

Body Paragraph #2 – 20 points

Topic sentence	3
Topic sentence starts with a clause	1
Topic sentence addresses second main idea	1
Describe using sensory descriptions	3
Make a comparison	3
Explain a cause/effect	3
Use three different transition words	3
Closing sentence	2
Closing sentence uses a different clause	1

Body Paragraph #3 – 20 points

Topic sentence	3
Topic sentence starts with a preposition	1
Topic sentence addresses third main idea	1
Describe using sensory descriptions	3
Make a comparison	3
Explain a cause/effect	3
Use three different transition words	3
Closing sentence	2
Closing sentence uses another preposition	1

Closing Paragraph – 20 points

Answer three questions from opening	6
Restate topic in different words	3
Thesis restates your reaction to the changes	3
Main idea – list three details	6
Clincher – one line about what you've learned	2

Rubric: Analytic

	Above Average (4)	Sufficient (3)	Developing (2)	Needs Improvement (1)
Introduces the topic clearly				
Develops the topic with relevant facts, definitions, concrete details, quotations, or other information and examples				
Uses appropriate transitions to create cohesion and clarifies the relationships among ideas and concepts				
Uses precise language and domain-specific vocabulary to inform about or explain the topic				
Establishes and maintains a formal style				
Provides a concluding statement or section that follows from and supports the information or explanation presented				
Produces clear and coherent writing in which the development, organization, and style are appropriate to task, purpose, and audience				
Develops and strengthens writing as needed by planning, revising, editing, rewriting, or trying a new approach, focusing on how well purpose and audience have been addressed				
Uses technology, including the Internet, to produce and publish writing; and links to and cites sources				
Draws evidence from literary or informational texts to support analysis, reflection, and research				

Rubric: Holistic

4	The student writes an exemplary informative/explanatory text that examines a topic and conveys ideas, concepts, and information through the selection, organization, and analysis of relevant content. The topic is clearly introduced and a variety of strategies are used to support the thesis. Supporting details are distinct and varied. Transitions are logical and smooth, and there are minimal grammatical or mechanical errors.
3	The student writes an effective informative/explanatory text that examines a topic and conveys ideas, concepts, and information through the selection, organization, and analysis of relevant content. The topic is adequately introduced and a few strategies are used to support the thesis. There are relevant supporting details. Transitions are logical, and grammatical or mechanical errors do not interfere with meaning.
2	The purpose and topic of the informative/explanatory text are not clearly identified. Some information is logically selected but not well organized or organized loosely. Analysis of relevant content is superficial. There is little variety in the strategies used to support the thesis. Supporting details are minimal and obvious or superficial. Transitions are not effective or are missing. There are noticeable grammatical or mechanical errors.
1	The topic of the informative/explanatory texts is unclear or lacking. The student does not present ideas, concepts, and information in a relevant or organized way. There are few or no supporting details and no transitions. Grammatical or mechanical errors are frequent and distract from the ability to comprehend the work.

(Adapted from *Assessment: Types of Rubrics*, DePaul University)

Chapter 4

Argument Text

Overview of the Genre

Purpose

An argument is used to persuade or convince. This can be done in a number of ways, which means the student has to be able to decide which way is the best way in each specific circumstance. There are two key pieces of information that a student must consider when writing an argument: the topic or reason for writing and the audience.

The topic or reason for writing gives students a basis for a format. If the topic is something political, the format may be something formal, such as an address, an essay, or a declaration. If the topic is more commercial in approach, the format may be more relaxed, maybe involving humor or interesting visuals with strong associative powers. If the reason for writing is to try to suggest a solutions to a problem, the format may be a newspaper editorial. If the reason for writing is to shed light on a serious social issue, the format may be a fictional satire. Before writing an argument piece, the author must understand the characteristics of each of these formats so he or she can make an informed decision about which format will be best suited to the topic.

Audience

The author must then also consider the audience for the piece. Understanding the likely recipients will determine the tone of the piece as well as the word choice. If the topic is something political, the audience will probably be voting adults. Therefore, the tone should be serious and the word choice somewhat intellectual. If the topic is commercial, the audience will most likely be younger consumers, so the tone may be humorous and the word choice may lean toward the colloquial or even slang. If suggesting a solution to a problem, the audience may be the authoritative power, in which case the tone should be reverential and the word choice respectful. If the topic is a serious social issue, the audience may be the author's peers, in which case the tone could be conversational and the word choice emotional.

Having a strong grasp of the components of argument text will help students make better choices when they write an argument and critically analyze persuasive writing when they read one. Argument text has many of the same characteristics as explanatory text: a strong organizational structure, main ideas and supporting details, and an evocative conclusion. What distinguishes argument text from explanatory or informational text, though, is the types of details that are used to support the main points.

Reading Strategy: Asking Questions

Focus: Propaganda Techniques

Propaganda techniques show up in politics, but they also can be found in advertising, editorials, reviews, and fiction. Propaganda can take many forms: words, visuals, statistics, and even technology. Students will need to understand different ways to manipulate an audience so they can recognize these methods when they read and use them when they write. To do this, students must be critical thinkers and readers who question what they read.

Propaganda techniques can be identified as bandwagon ("everyone else is doing it"), authoritative ("four out of five doctors say..."), testimonial ("a celebrity believes..."), name-calling ("you don't want to be thought of as..."), facts left out ("drinking coffee will make you smarter..."), opinions as facts ("world's best hot dog"), or misleading red herrings ("this detergent leaves your clothes smelling fresh"). By asking questions as they read, students will start to think about underlying or subtle shades of meaning. Seeking answers to those questions gives students a purpose for reading and, more important, gives them the practice they need in doing a close reading and scrutinizing the language of the text they read. In a 21st century world where access to information is immediate, students need to cultivate their questioning skills so they can validate the credibility of the information they read.

Reading Strategy: Inferring

As a reader, students need to be aware of audience, tone, and word choice in order to identify two types of propaganda techniques: emotional and logical. Authors will try many tactics to create an inference in the mind of the reader. An inference is made when the clues in the text combined with the personal experiences of the reader lead to an unstated outcome. An awareness of how language can be manipulated is only possible when students make inferences from the text and determine whether they are getting the true message that was intended.

Focus: Emotion

Emotional techniques play on an audience's fears, hopes, worries, or joys. Tapping into an emotional connection will tie a reader to a point of view, even if the reader can't exactly explain why. Recently my 15-year-old son was listening to my iPod in the car when a song came on that was the lullaby we used to sing to him as a baby. All of a sudden, he started crying uncontrollably and he had no idea why. Emotions run deep and can be long lasting. Opening up that floodgate can inspire great and long-lasting loyalty.

When they read, students should look for high-impact terms, such as *honor, love, loyalty, guilt,* and *fear.* Students should also pay attention to pictures and illustrations, which can portray strong emotions without any words. Imagine seeing a picture of a baby laughing or a puppy caught in a cage. Each of these images will evoke powerful feelings that will sway our opinions.

Focus: Logic

Logical techniques, on the other hand, rely on the reader's desire to be logical. Statistics can be a powerful form of convincing propaganda because people tend to believe that numbers don't lie. But readers must be careful that the statistics tell the whole story. Statistics can be misleading, especially if information is left out or not objectively represented. Students need practice analyzing statistics with a critical eye. They need to ask good questions to see whether all the information has been included and what may have been left out. This requires students to read between the lines and fill in missing information or at least to be aware that information may be missing.

False logic is another way to be persuasive. This is when a statement seems to make perfect sense but, in reality, the foundation of the argument is flawed and therefore not valid. Students must be able to trace an argument backward to its logical beginning and make sure that all the reasoning was valid.

Prerequisite Skills

Because this unit will focus on the reading strategies of making connections and inferring, students will need practice with these tools. Provide Mini-Lessons that ask students to recall ads they have seen or their favorite commercials. Ask students how they persuade their parents to give them something they want or how they convince a younger sibling to do something. What is different about their approaches, and why do they use different techniques in different situations?

Have students practice recognizing the clues necessary to make good predictions, and show how to make inferences by integrating your own personal experiences with the stated clues to read between the lines.

Academic Vocabulary

In argument especially, words will have subtle shades of meaning. Give students exposure to various contexts for common academic terms to help them be comfortable seeing the shades of meaning and ambiguity of certain words. Such ambiguity will matter when every word counts.

During reading, students may still encounter unknown words, so it is important to teach them decoding strategies as well. Some decoding strategies they can use during reading include:

- Looking at the context to determine what the word probably means.
- Seeing if the word is defined in the text by an example or a non-example.
- Looking at the root words to determine the meaning.
- Determining the part of speech to understand how the word is being used.

Sample Planning Calendar

Decide on a culminating assignment (some ideas are provided across content areas at the end of this section on page 117). Enter the due date for this project at the end of the third week or the beginning of the fourth week of instruction. Work backward to introduce reading and writing instruction and guided practice opportunities. Allow time for comprehension checks, Mini-Lessons, re-teaching, and test prep. A sample of a four-week unit on argument writing appears below.

Monday	Tuesday	Wednesday	Thursday	Friday
RI: Persuasive Techniques – Propaganda	RP: Persuasive Techniques – Propaganda	WI: Persuasive Techniques – Propaganda	WP: Persuasive Techniques – Propaganda	RI/WP: Emotion vs. Logic V: Descriptive Verbs
RI: Making Connections	RP: Emotion vs. Logic WI: Quotes	RI: Text Structures WI: Call to Action V: Infinitives and Imperatives	RP: Text Structures WP: Call to Action	RP: Text Structures G: Parallel Structures
RI: Testimonial	RP: Testimonial WI: Supporting Details G: Punctuation for Quotes	WP: Supporting Details WI: Openings and Closings	RI: Word Choice WI: Cohesive Word Choices G: Active vs. Passive Voice	WP: Drafting Culminating Project (optional placement)
WP: Revising Culminating Project (optional placement)	RP: Comprehension Check	WP: Editing G: Quotes, Parallel Structures, Active Voice TEST PREP	TEST PREP	TEST PREP

Legend

RI = Reading Instruction
RP = Reading Practice
WI = Writing Instruction
WP = Writing Practice
V   = Vocabulary
G   = Grammar

Writing Strategy Overview: Be Convincing!

Many students practice the art of persuasion every day without even realizing it. They convince their parents to let them stay up late or go to a movie, they convince their friends to join them for an adventure, or they convince their teachers to forgive a tardy. Once students recognize the techniques of effective persuasion, they can practice using it more effectively.

Persuasion and argument is one text type that students are more intrinsically motivated to learn. Adolescents are naturally argumentative, and this genre capitalizes on their innate abilities. Note: The term *argument* is defined here as "a claim that is to be supported by evidence." This term should not be defined as "a confrontation."

In this section, students will practice using logical and emotional appeals in their writing. They will learn to recognize the elements of these types of persuasion not only in text, but in pictures, videos, and music as well. Through guided prewriting activities, students will see the advantages and disadvantages of each type of persuasion. As they begin to write drafts, they will see how using their understanding of audience, purpose, and tone can and should influence their word choices and contribute to a cohesive argument. Finally, they will see how to revise their work with richer vocabulary and interesting sentence structures.

Consider giving students a culminating project that requires them to apply all their new skills in an integrated way. By studying and practicing the art of argument, students will gain confidence in critical thinking.

Prewriting Mini-Lesson: Logical Appeals

Common Core State Standard

Write arguments to support claims with clear reasons and relevant evidence. Support claim(s) with logical reasoning and relevant evidence, using accurate, credible sources and demonstrating an understanding of the topic or text.

Materials

- Copy of a logic problem
- Chart paper
- Graph paper
- Reading and Writing Portfolio
- *Text Types and Purposes Reference Sheet,* page 20
- *Data Analysis* recording sheet, page 97
- Set of six *ESP Cards* for each pair of students (each card has a different shape on it: star, circle, moon, triangle, etc.), page 98

Overview

Students will use data and deductive reasoning to try to convince or persuade.

Planning

There are many free logic problems for all skill levels to be found on the Internet or in puzzle books. Prepare enough *ESP Cards* for each pair of students. Allow time for students to record their data.

Procedure

Modeling

1. Introduce the word *logic*. Tell students that we tend to find logic very believable and convincing because it appeals to our rational selves.

2. Distribute copies of a simple logic problem and display a copy of the logic problem on the board. Guide students to solve the problem by using the chart paper. Explain that *deductive reasoning* means eliminating choices.

3. Have students turn to a partner and discuss why deductive reasoning is convincing. Ask students to share their answers, and post their responses on the chart paper to display.

4. On another sheet of chart paper, write the word *data*. Explain to students that data is another way to be persuasive because it represents factual information that was gathered firsthand.

5. Tell students they will have an opportunity to gather some data firsthand themselves.

Guided Practice

6. Distribute the *Data Analysis* recording sheets and one set of *ESP Cards* for each pair of students. Ask students whether they believe in Extrasensory Perception (ESP), which is the ability to read someone's mind or see the future. Tell students they will use data to determine whether ESP is real.

7. Have students work together to test their ESP by following the directions on the *Data Analysis* recording sheets. Have students work together for about 15 minutes. Tell students not to share the tally until the end of the round.

8. Ask the class what kind of data they were able to gather. Have them brainstorm ways to show their data (e.g., using a graph, table, or chart).
9. Distribute graph paper or chart paper to each pair and have them display their findings graphically.

Independent Practice

10. Have students post their charts. Then, ask them to examine all the charts and come to a conclusion.
11. Tell students to write a paragraph arguing that ESP is real. Have students refer to the data they collected to prove their points.

Reading Connection

Tell students that data only gives part of the story and can be manipulated. Have students read text that uses false logic or faulty data, or show a graph that only reveals part of a story. Ask students to imagine various ways to fill in the blanks. How would the argument change with the new information? Model how to summarize an argument with new information, and challenge students to use this strategy when they watch the news, read an article in a newspaper, view a commercial, or listen to a speech. Have students highlight examples of both faulty and valid logic that they find in their reading and keep track of these examples by listing them in their Reading and Writing Portfolios.

Formative Assessment

If the student...	Consider practicing these prerequisite skills:
had trouble reading data	graphs and tables
had trouble solving deductive reasoning problems	math puzzles and riddles

Logical Appeals

Name:_____

Data Analysis

Directions: Work with a partner. Select one ESP Card. Have your partner guess the shape. Write a checkmark each time your partner guesses the correct shape. Tally the scores and plot them on a graph using graph or chart paper.

Round 1		Round 2		Round 3	
Partner A	**Partner B**	**Partner A**	**Partner B**	**Partner A**	**Partner B**

Total: _____   _____   _____   _____   _____   _____

ESP Cards

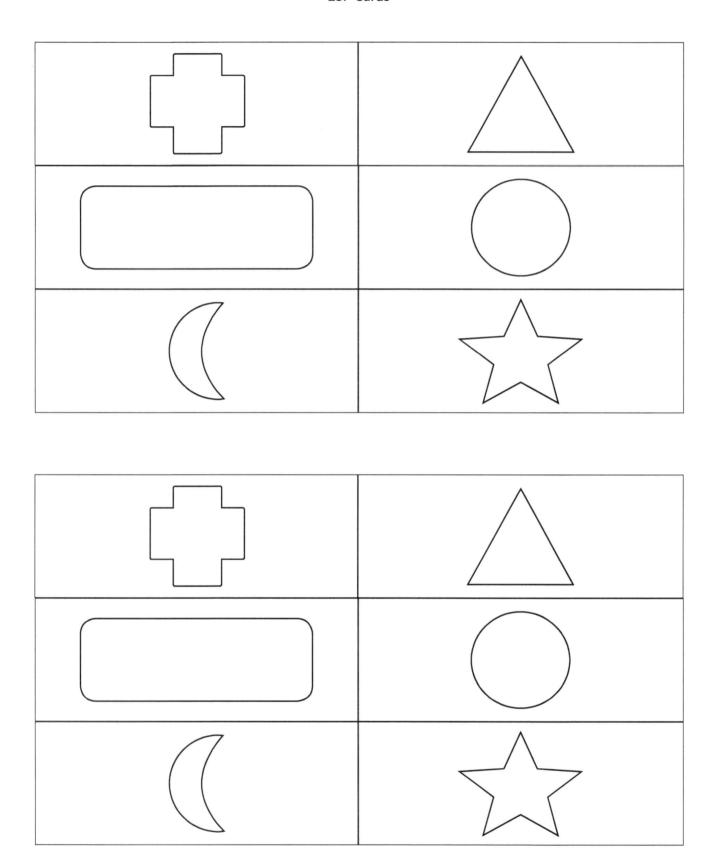

Prewriting Mini-Lesson: Emotional Appeals

Common Core State Standard

Write arguments to support claims with clear reasons and relevant evidence. Introduce claim(s), acknowledge alternate or opposing claims, and organize the reasons and evidence logically.

Materials

- Chart paper
- Several magazine ads, each portraying one propaganda technique
- Sticky notes
- Colored highlighter tape
- *Propaganda* activity sheet, page 101

Overview

Students will learn to identify types of emotional persuasion, including propaganda techniques, by analyzing magazine ads.

Planning

Find at least one magazine ad for each propaganda technique. Use additional ads for the activity sheets.

Procedure

Modeling

1. Introduce the word *propaganda*. Explain to students that propaganda is a form of persuasion because it plays with your emotions.
2. Ask students why emotions can be a powerful persuasive tool. (*Emotions make us act without thinking.*) Have students brainstorm some strong emotions. Write their responses on chart paper.
3. Make a concept map by choosing one emotion (e.g., fear) and listing all the characteristics associated with that emotion (e.g., anxiety, worry, stress, and panic).
4. Distribute copies of the *Propaganda* activity sheet to students. Discuss each type of emotional appeal. Have students summarize your descriptions into three bullet points per technique.

Guided Practice

5. Have students work in groups. Post the magazine pictures around the room. Have students initial their sticky notes and place them on the picture they feel best represents that persuasive technique.
6. After all students have had a chance to add a sticky note to each picture, have them sit down and tally the responses.
7. Have students share their reasoning.

Independent Practice

8. Have students find one advertisement from a magazine, a newspaper, or the Internet. Ask students to write a paragraph describing a.) the propaganda technique used and b.) the specific elements and characteristics of the ad that play on the audience's emotions.

Reading Connection

Give students two disparate pieces of text that rely on emotional appeals, such as an excerpt from a Winston Churchill speech and an excerpt from a speech by Adolf Hitler. Ask students to identify the specific language that plays on emotions. Have them use colored highlighter tape to call out various types of emotion that are expressed, such as yellow tape for fear-inspiring words or blue tape for hopeful words. Or use political speeches from two opposing candidates, and compare the kinds of appeals each candidate made. Ask students which type of appeal is most effective and why.

Formative Assessment

If the student...	Consider practicing these prerequisite skills:
had trouble identifying propaganda techniques	use images to help students identify strong emotions
had trouble distinguishing different types of emotions	have students explain causes and effects of different feelings

Emotional Appeals

Name:_____

Propaganda

Directions: Work with a partner. Look at the pictures and decide which propaganda technique is being used in each one. Use a sticky note to place that number on the picture, along with your name or initials.

1. Bandwagon "Everyone is doing it." • _____ • _____ • _____	**2. Testimonial** "The surgeon general warns that smoking is dangerous." • _____ • _____ • _____
3. Name-calling "The leading brand of furniture polish leaves a film on your table but not our brand!" • _____ • _____ • _____	**4. Black-and-White Fallacy** "Either buy this new computer or be stuck in the Dark Ages." • _____ • _____ • _____
5. Repetition "Two, two, two tastes in one." • _____ • _____ • _____	**6. Transfer** "Jennifer Hudson lost 40 pounds using our weight-loss program." • _____ • _____ • _____
7. Emotional Words "Tell her how much she means to you with diamonds." • _____ • _____ • _____	**8. Missing Data** "Buy this cell phone for just $4.99 (restrictions apply)." • _____ • _____ • _____

Writing Strategy Overview: Audience, Tone, and Purpose

Never underestimate the importance of knowing your audience. Nothing can derail a presentation faster than failing to understand the intended recipients and their expectations. Consider this hypothetical situation. You paid for a ticket to a fictional movie called *The Nightmare*. Most likely, you expected to see a horror film. The title of the movie created an image in your mind, a presupposition, that you are about to see a scary movie. However, the movie is a documentary about clinical psychologists who document children's dreams. This is a very different movie! Chances are the typical moviegoer would be very disappointed and unlikely to sit through this movie. Just as it's important to set the stage for moviegoers by using an appropriate title, it's important for writers to know their audience.

Once writers know their audience, they are better able to make decisions about the tone they will take (respectful, funny, formal, casual) and the words they will use (colloquial, academic, jargon, emotion-laden). The first Mini-Lesson will show students how to use their understanding of audience to choose a tone and make strong word decisions.

Understanding the audience is only one piece of the puzzle. Writers also must have a clear sense of the purpose of their writing. What is the outcome they're hoping to accomplish as a result of this writing? If writers want to offer a solution, they will first need to present and explain the problem. If they are trying to change someone's mind, they must first outline the flaws in that person's current point of view. If they are trying to sway others to their side of an issue, they will need to make their stance so appealing that people are happy and eager to jump on board.

Understanding the purpose helps writers make another choice about their writing. It helps them decide on the structure. How will they best present the information? Take the coach of a football team that is behind by one touchdown in the fourth quarter: His tactic for persuading the team to run the ball is going to be direct and strong. But if the coach is at a practice early in the season, his approach might be more drawn out, offering clear rationales and addressing the pros and cons of each play option. Recognizing the purpose helps writers take the most appropriate approach.

Drafting Mini-Lesson: Thematic Writing

Common Core State Standard

Use words, phrases, and clauses to create cohesion and clarify the relationships among claim(s), reasons, and evidence.

Materials

- Chart paper
- *Theme Restaurant* activity sheet, page 105

Overview

Students will imagine a theme restaurant and brainstorm terms that support the theme.

Planning

Consider using this activity to launch a culminating project. After students brainstorm ideas for their theme restaurant, ask them to use the elements of argument writing to create a commercial for their restaurant, including a poster with ad copy.

Procedure

Modeling

1. Introduce the word *thematic.* Ask students what they think it means, and have them give some examples. Write their ideas on a sheet of chart paper and display.

2. Explain to students that we see evidence of themes all around us. For example, many students have experienced a theme birthday party. Ask students to share examples of a theme party they have attended. What were some of the details that contributed to the theme? What was the effect? Add some of their comments to the chart paper.

3. Introduce the word *cohesive.* Tell students that just as a party is more cohesive when a theme is carried through, writing is also more cohesive when all the components support the theme.

Guided Practice

4. Have students work with partners or in small groups. Distribute copies of the *Themed Restaurant* activity sheet to students.

5. Instruct students to choose a theme for an imaginary restaurant. Have them write their theme choice on their activity sheets.

6. Next, ask students to work together to think of all the specific terminology that is associated with that theme. For example, if they were to create a surfing-themed restaurant, students might add terms like *hang ten, catch a wave, shred,* or *surf's up.*

7. Tell students to sort the terms by the part of speech indicated on their activity sheets.

Independent Practice

8. Ask students to use the sentence starter on their activity sheets to write a brief description of their restaurant and to create a menu. Challenge them to use all the terms they came up with in their descriptions and to also use those terms to name the individual dishes.

Reading Connection

Ask students to read an article from the sports page or the entertainment section in the newspaper. Articles from these sections are often filled with strong thematic elements. Have them identify the topic of the article and then circle or highlight the words that contribute to the cohesiveness of the piece. Have them replace those words with more generic terms and then reread the article and discuss how the tone of the article changed.

Formative Assessment

If the student...	Consider practicing these prerequisite skills:
had trouble thinking of enough terminology	start with a broader, more general theme
had trouble coming up with a theme	list sports, types of movies, or names of countries, and describe the specific characteristics of each

Thematic Writing

Name:_____

Theme Restaurant

Directions: Imagine you are creating a theme restaurant. Write the theme of your restaurant below. Then, use the chart to brainstorm terms related to your theme. Sort the terms by their part of speech. Finally, write a brief description of your restaurant, and create a menu using the terms you selected to name each dish.

Theme:

Brainstorm Terminology:			
Verbs	**Nouns**	**Adjectives**	**Adverbs**

Welcome to _____ Restaurant!

_____

_____

_____

_____

_____

_____

Menu:

Drafting Mini-Lesson: A Strong Foundation

Common Core State Standard

Introduce claim(s), acknowledge alternate or opposing claims, and organize the reasons and evidence logically.

Materials

- Clear, plastic drinking cups labeled "Yes" and "No"
- Cotton balls
- Sugar cubes
- Reading and Writing Portfolio
- *Balanced Argument* activity sheet, page 108
- *Supporting Details Cube* template, page 109

Overview

Students will understand the importance of creating a balanced argument, and they will learn two ways they can structure an argument paper, depending on the purpose of the argument.

Planning

Plates or clear bags may be used in place of the cups. The containers should be large enough to hold several cotton balls.

Procedure

Modeling

1. Explain to students that there are many reasons to argue. Today they will learn about two of them.

2. Some arguments are about winning. The goal is to convince an audience that you are right. This type of argument is characterized by having two sides. On a sheet of chart paper, write "WIN." Ask students for some examples of arguments that involve winning, and write their ideas on the chart paper.

3. An argument is similar to a sports match in that the writer must present the points for each side and show clearly that the side with the most or the best points "wins" the argument. (Note: The fact that one side offers more points or more rational does not necessarily mean it should "win.")

4. Ask a student volunteer to come to the front of the room to help you demonstrate a balanced argument.

5. Give the student two cups to hold, one in each hand. Choose a topic that is relevant to students, such as curfew. Ask students to brainstorm reasons why curfew should be enforced. For every reason they give, place one cotton ball in the "Yes" cup.

6. Next, ask students to brainstorm reasons why curfew should not be enforced. For each reason they give, place one cotton ball in the "No" cup.

7. Ask students which argument was more convincing. Students should see that one side has more reasons than the other.

8. Distribute copies of the *Balanced Argument* activity sheet to students. Have students work with partners, and give each pair of students one set of two cups and several cotton balls.

9. Ask students to choose one topic from the activity sheet. Have students work together to come up with reasons *for* or *against* the argument. Have them add one cotton ball to the cup each time they think of a reason.

10. Next, tell students that besides having enough points to win an argument, the points must be strong and supported. Distribute sugar cubes to each pair of students.

11. Ask students to build two pyramids—one from sugar cubes, and one from cotton balls. Which pyramid is stronger?

12. Tell students that the sugar cube pyramid is stronger because the sugar cubes are solid, with many sides that create a sturdy foundation to add more sugar cubes. Cotton balls are too flimsy to build upon. Similarly, their arguments will be stronger when they add more details and dimension.

Independent Practice

13. Ask students to choose the best three arguments from either the "Yes" or the "No" side of their activity sheets. Have them support each argument with six examples. For their supporting details, students can use their Reading and Writing Portfolios and refer to the explanatory techniques of supporting a main idea by offering a description or definition, making a prediction, providing a comparison, or showing a cause and effect. For the last two details, students should choose two propaganda techniques.

14. Distribute copies of the *Supporting Details Cube* template to students. Ask students to record six details in the cube. When the cube is complete, they can build it, roll it, and discuss what they wrote with a partner.

Reading Connection

As students are reading persuasive or argumentative text, have them identify the pro and con arguments by looking for key words, such as *argue, refute, judge, conclude, sum up,* or *decide.* Have them sort the arguments and align the counterarguments. Then, have them decide whether the argument was effectively won or lost. As an extension activity, have students add their own arguments to a losing side to see if they can make that argument stronger.

Formative Assessment

If the student...	Consider practicing these prerequisite skills:
had trouble supporting his or her arguments	review supporting details from the explanatory chapter
had trouble thinking of propaganda techniques	review logical and emotional appeals

A Strong Foundation

Name:_____

Balanced Argument

Directions: Choose one topic from the topic bank below. Work with a partner to compile a list of reasons that support the topic ("Yes") and a list of reasons that oppose the topic ("No").

Topic Bank

Abolish the dress code   Lower the voting age to 16   Do away with grades

Cheerleading is not a sport   Ban certain books from the library

Think of your own topic!

Yes   **No**

_____   _____

_____   _____

_____   _____

_____   _____

_____   _____

_____   _____

Which side won?

_____

A Strong Foundation

Supporting Details Cube

Directions: Choose one reason, either for or against something. Write six supporting details on the cube template. Use the choices below to help you write supporting details. Roll finished cubes with a partner and explain the roll.

Describe/define

Show a cause and effect

Compare or contrast

Make a prediction

Use an emotional propaganda technique

Use a logical propaganda technique

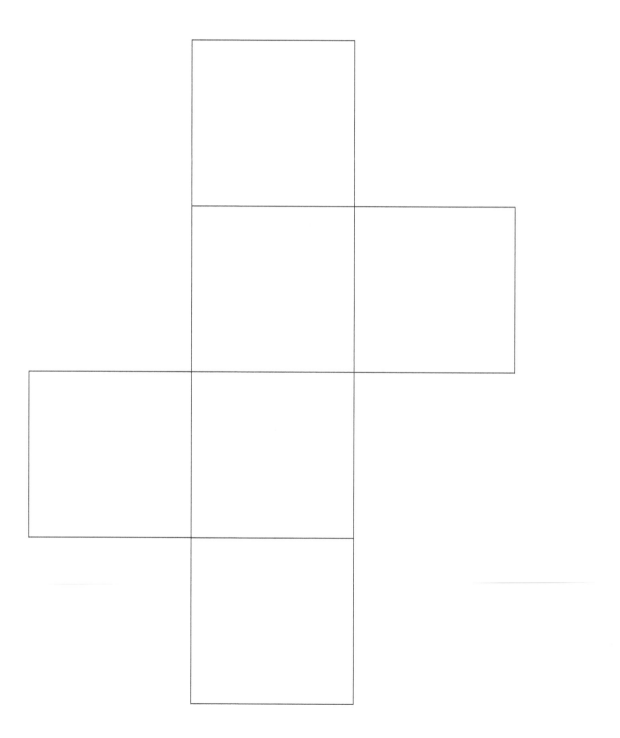

Writing Strategy Overview: Fortify Your Writing

There is a tendency among young writers to overuse the passive voice. The passive voice implies a tone of resignation, of compromise, and of acquiescence. These are not necessarily bad qualities, but they aren't the attention-getting characteristics of a persuasive argument.

Part of the revising process, then, should ask students to look closely at the voice in the essay. A passive voice makes a weak argument, but an active voice, using imperative and descriptive verbs, will set a clear and forceful tone.

In addition, the structure of an argument can weaken or strengthen its impact. Just as a stool is sturdier on three legs than on two, an essay should be built so that the foundation is as concrete as possible. Build an argument with a weak foundation, and it will be easy to poke holes and topple the piece through simple counterclaims. By rearranging their supporting evidence, students can fortify their essays and place the most substantial pieces of evidence front and center, creating a fortress for their thoughts.

Revising Mini-Lesson: Grammar

Common Core State Standard
Establish and maintain a formal style.

Materials
- Chart paper
- Reading and Writing Portfolios
- *Text Types and Purposes Reference Sheet,* page 20
- *Loud and Strong* activity sheet, page 113

Overview
Students will practice using the imperative form of verbs to express their ideas.

Planning
Create a list of passive verbs and expressions to distribute to students. They can use their *Text Types and Purposes Reference Sheets* to refer to, and have them create a pocket in their Reading and Writing Portfolios for collecting examples of imperatives.

Procedure
Modeling

1. Ask students to brainstorm a list of commands they might give their dog. Write their ideas on a sheet of chart paper.

2. Ask students what all these commands have in common (*commands are usually written in the imperative*). Introduce the term *imperative*. Explain that it means *extremely important*, but that it also describes a type of verb. It means a verb that is written as a one-word command, such as "Stop!" A one-word command is stronger and more attention-grabbing than a long, passive statement that takes too long to get to the point.

3. Tell students that one strong characteristic of argument writing is the use of strong, sure language, including imperatives. Tell students they will practice turning long, passive phrases into imperatives.

Guided Practice

4. Have students work with partners or in small groups. Distribute copies of the *Loud and Strong* activity sheet to each pair or group.

5. Students will work together to choose passive sentences and change the passive tone to an imperative tone. Then, they will create road signs using the strong imperative statements.

Independent Practice

6. Ask students to collect examples of passive phrases they find on television, in the newspaper, or in magazines. Have them use an online word-cloud generator, such as Wordle, to import the phrases and see how they look when converted into a visual collage.

7. Ask students to rewrite the phrases into imperative phrases and convert that text using a word-cloud generator. What do they notice? Have students write a paragraph about the difference between passive and imperative voice.

Reading Connection

As students read persuasive text, have them list the examples of imperative words they find in their Reading and Writing Portfolios. Have them connect these words with emotions by writing how each word makes them feel. Challenge them to consider why an author might choose a strong, imperative sentence versus a passive statement. What impact does each have on the text as a whole?

Formative Assessment

If the student...	Consider practicing these prerequisite skills:
had trouble thinking of imperatives	review commands
had trouble seeing the difference between passive and active voice	review linking verbs and clauses

Grammar

Name:_____

Loud and Strong

Directions: Read the sentences in the Sentence Bank below. Rewrite each to an imperative. Choose one sentence to turn into a road sign.

Sentence Bank

It might be a good idea to move at a more leisurely pace.

Moving faster by speeding up is one way to get to a place more quickly.

It would be best to embark on the journey soon.

The thing that is happening now should be avoided and prevented from happening again.

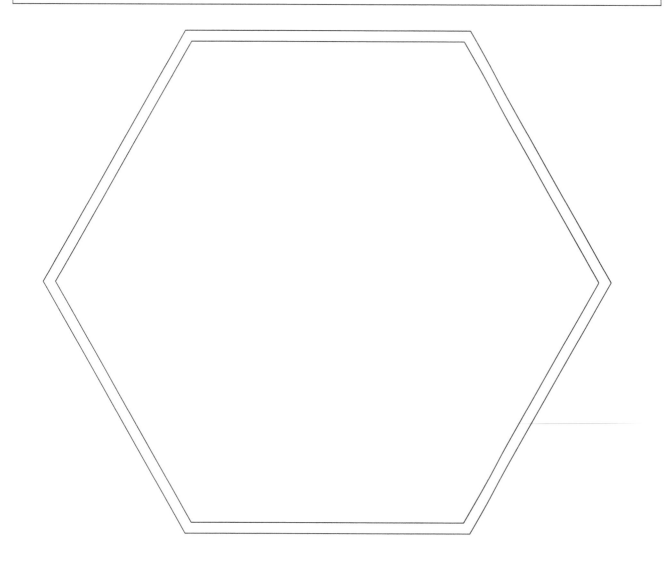

Revising Mini-Lesson: Form and Function

Common Core State Standard

Support claim(s) with logical reasoning and relevant evidence, using accurate, credible sources and demonstrating an understanding of the topic or text.

Materials

- Tangram shapes created from laminated cardstock
- *Build Your Own Structure* activity sheet, page 116

Overview

Students will create sculptures to represent ways to structure an argumentative piece.

Planning

Use cardstock to create basic tangram shapes, including squares, rectangles, hexagons, and triangles. Laminate the cardstock so students can use dry-erase markers to write on them multiple times.

Procedure

Modeling

1. Tell students there are many ways to structure an argument. They can start with their most important point first and conclude with the weakest argument. Or they can start with the weakest argument and conclude with the strongest. Alternatively, they can offer two clearly opposing viewpoints by focusing on one viewpoint first and then the other and concluding with a paragraph that offers a decision about which viewpoint is best.

2. Tell students that one format is not necessarily better than another. What matters is that once they decide on a format, they use it consistently and structure their writing around it.

Guided Practice

3. Distribute copies of the *Build Your Own Structure* activity sheet and a set of tangrams to students.

4. Have students use the tangrams to create a visual representation of the three composition structures described on the activity sheets. Have them draw each interpretation next to the description.

5. Ask students to label each shape as the opening, closing, argument, counterargument, or supporting detail.

Independent Practice

6. Assign a topic to students and have them write an argument either for or against it. Instruct students to use one of the structures they created.

7. Tell students to be prepared to explain how their structure was organized, or ask students to write a description in their Reading and Writing Portfolios.

Reading Connection

Have students use the tangram shapes while they read, and challenge them to determine the structures of the passages they read. Students can label the tangrams with different components as necessary.

Formative Assessment

If the student...	Consider practicing this prerequisite skill:
had trouble creating structures	order of importance

Form and Function

Name:_____

Build Your Own Structure

Directions: Use the tangrams your teacher gave you to create a visual representation of each structure described below. Draw your representation next to the description, and label each shape.

1. Introduction, argument, supporting details, counterargument, supporting details, conclusion

2. Introduction, weakest argument, supporting details, stronger argument, supporting details, strongest argument, supporting details, conclusion

3. Introduction, strongest argument, supporting details, weaker argument, supporting details, weakest argument, supporting details, conclusion

Culminating Project Ideas

Language Arts

Invent a theme restaurant, and create an advertisement (video, print, or radio spot) to convince patrons to dine there.

Suggested mentor texts: *The Adventures of Tom Sawyer* by Mark Twain; "Blood, Toil, Tears and Sweat: Address to Parliament on May 13th, 1940" by Winston Churchill

Social Studies

Collaborate with a group to write a constitution that addresses a grievance you may have about your school or classroom.

Suggested mentor texts: *Preamble and First Amendment to the United States Constitution; The Words We Live By: Your Annotated Guide to the Constitution* by Linda R. Monk

Mathematics

Review a series of surveys about social issues, shopping, food choices, etc., and choose a graph that is most appropriate to display the results. Present your data and use it to make a persuasive argument about what you learned from the data.

Suggested mentor text: *Geeks: How Two Lost Boys Rode the Internet out of Idaho* by Jon Katz

Science

Use satellite tools, such as Google Earth, to examine a change that has occurred over time, such as the effect of deforestation of the rain forest or the changes in polar ice. Document the changes and write a letter to a university convincing scholars to investigate the phenomenon.

Suggested mentor text: "Geology" *(U*X*L Encyclopedia of Science)*

Additional Resources

Essay Frames

I. OPENING PARAGRAPH

Who is your **audience**?

_____

What is your **tone**?

_____

INFER! What is the bigger issue?

_____

(START YOUR ESSAY ROUGH DRAFT HERE)

Write **three grabber questions:**

1.

2.

3.

State the **topic:**

_____

Thesis: How do you feel about this topic?

_____

_____

Main Ideas:

Whom are you addressing?

_____

What is it you want to achieve?

_____

What will your audience get out of it?

_____

_____

II. BODY PARAGRAPH

1. Address your audience and choose your tone through word choice. Start this sentence with an **imperative**:

_____

a. Explain the situation: What are you trying to achieve?

_____

_____

_____

_____

b. Predict/infer: Use a propaganda technique to persuade your audience to do what you want.

_____

_____

_____

c. Show cause and effect: Tell your reader what he/she will gain by going along with your idea.

_____

_____

_____

2. Closing sentence: Use another imperative, and reiterate in strong words why your idea is good.

_____

_____

HOMEWORK: USE THIS WORKSHEET TO WRITE YOUR BODY PARAGRAPHS, DUE TOMORROW!

III. CLOSING PARAGRAPH

Answer the three grabber questions:

1.

2.

3.

Restate the topic, substituting different words:

_____

_____

_____

Restate the thesis:

_____

_____

Restate details from the main ideas:

_____

_____

_____

Clincher: End with a warning or a friendly reminder (decide based on tone):

_____

_____

Use this warning/reminder as your title:

_____

_____

Rubric: Point-based

Format – 20 points

Five paragraphs (introduction, three body paragraphs, conclusion)	5
Typed or handwritten in ink	5
Proper paragraphs	5
Spelling/punctuation	5

Opening Paragraph – 25 points

Title matches clincher	5
Three grabber questions, address category	7
Topic	3
Thesis	4
Main ideas	6

Body Paragraph – 50 points

Topic sentence	10
Topic sentence uses imperative	3
Imperative matches audience/tone	2
Explain	10
Use a propaganda technique	10
Cause/effect	10
Closing sentence	3
Closing sentence uses another imperative	2

Closing Paragraph – 25 points

Answer three grabber questions	6
Restate topic	4
Restate thesis	4
Restate main ideas	6
Clincher	5

Rubric: Analytic

	Above Average (4)	Sufficient (3)	Developing (2)	Needs Improvement (1)
Introduces claim(s), acknowledges alternate or opposing claims, and organizes the reasons and evidence logically				
Supports claim(s) with logical reasoning and relevant evidence, using accurate, credible sources and demonstrating an understanding of the topic or text				
Uses words, phrases, and clauses to create cohesion and clarifies the relationships among claim(s), reasons, and evidence				
Establishes and maintains a formal style				
Provides a concluding statement or section that follows from and supports the argument presented				
Produces clear and coherent writing in which the development, organization, and style are appropriate to task, purpose, and audience				
Develops and strengthens writing as needed by planning, revising, editing, rewriting, or trying a new approach, focusing on how well purpose and audience have been addressed				
Uses technology, including the Internet, to produce and publish writing; and links to and cites sources				
Draws evidence from literary or informational texts to support analysis, reflection, and research				
Traces and evaluates the argument and specific claims in a text, assessing whether the reasoning is sound and the evidence is relevant and sufficient to support the claims				

Rubric: Holistic

4	The student writes arguments to support claims with clear reasons and relevant evidence. The claim set forth is clearly identified and is supported by clear and relevant details, including logical and emotional appeals as appropriate to audience and tone. The organizational structure is strong and cohesive and informs the content. Mechanical or grammatical errors are minimal.
3	The claim is fairly clear and is supported by somewhat relevant details, including either logical or emotional appeals. Information is presented in a fairly logical and coherent manner. Minimal errors do not detract from overall meaning and understanding.
2	The claim is not clearly identified, and supporting evidence is not fully connected; or, only minimal and superficial amounts of evidence are presented as support, and the choice of logical versus emotional appeals is not transparent. The organization is present but is not thoughtful nor cohesive. There are several noticeable misspellings and mechanical errors.
1	The claim is unclear and a central idea is lacking. There is little related evidence to support the claim, and information is presented in a disorganized manner. Misspellings and mechanical errors are frequent and distract from the ability to comprehend the work.

(Adapted from *Assessment: Types of Rubrics*, DePaul University)

Chapter 5

Narrative Text

Overview of the Genre

Purpose

Narrative text relates a series of events, either real or invented. Mostly associated with storytelling, narrative can be a biography, a fictional account, or the relation of a historical incident.

Why do we tell stories? Stories help us learn about the world, the past, and other cultures. Ultimately, they help us understand ourselves. Seeing the universality of people's feelings, fears, hopes, and dreams connects us to others and shows us that we are not alone in the world. Common experiences unite people across time and space and help us understand one another with empathy and compassion.

A narrative is often viewed as the most natural form of writing for students, since it allows them to tell a story through their writing. Many teachers start the school year by asking students to write a personal narrative as a way to get to know them. College entrance exams and essays often require a personal narrative. This is because a narrative can be a terrific vehicle for self-reflection. There are two reasons narrative is introduced as the last genre in this book. First, writing a personal narrative can be a risky undertaking for a vulnerable adolescent. Writing is very revealing, and a student needs to feel safe and supported before he or she will consent to sharing inner thoughts and feelings. This safety takes time to cultivate and can be too much to ask at the beginning of a school year.

Second, as a text type, a narrative has the most liberal definition of structure. Since a story can be told in a variety of formats, a narrative may not the best way to introduce and reinforce specific structural features. Once students have a strong foundation of organizational skills, they are better equipped to experiment with and veer from a rigid format. Giving students lots of practice with specific structures arms them with choices and options for writing narratives later on.

Reading Strategy: Summarizing

Focus: Context

The goal of reading a narrative is to understand some universal truth. But to do this, a reader must have background information.

Start by examining the story in the context of the setting and point of view. The setting will provide information about the location, time period, time of year, and events going on around the story. The setting offers a frame to support the story and will help students make inferences about the theme of the story.

Next, recognize who is telling the story. The point of view of the narrator or main character is important, as it is the lens through which the reader experiences the events. Point of view can be very subjective, and students should start to realize that one event can be interpreted in many ways, depending on the point of view. Help students recognize the point of view and also analyze why the author chose that point of view. Was it to gain sympathy from the reader? Was it a way to put the reader in an uncomfortable position, to help him or her examine his or her own beliefs?

Focus: Conflict

A narrative can be characterized first by its structure. Whether the events are sequential, told in flashback, or some combination of these, there should be a logical progression from one event to the next. Typically, a narrative structure will have some common components.

The most basic narrative will begin with an introduction of the setting, the characters, and, most important, the conflict. The conflict is the element that elevates a narrative from a series of unrelated events to a thematic journey in which the character must overcome an obstacle, face a fear, or fulfill a quest. Once the conflict is established, the events drive the story to a climax (when the conflict is finally addressed) and a resolution (when the outcome is realized). The story concludes with the realization that something has changed for the character and that his or her life will forever be altered by the experiences recounted in the narrative.

Conflicts can be broadly characterized as man vs. man, man vs. self, or man vs. nature. Conflicts can then be made more specific, such as overcoming an obstacle or a physical handicap or trying to reach a goal. Students need to use summarizing strategies to keep track of the events as they occur and decide which events were small obstacles to overcome, which events represented the climax, and which events represented the resolution.

Reading Strategy: Making Connections

Focus: Allusions

We ask students to make personal connections when they read in order to activate prior knowledge and to help them get invested in the text. Authors help readers to do this by providing allusions. Allusions are deliberate references, overt or subtle, to another text, another story, a world event, or our own lives. They can show up in the form of literary devices, such as symbols or metaphors. They can also show up in the form of jokes. A great example of an allusion occurs in the Disney film *Toy Story*. There is a scene when the toys are driving the pink doll car through the toy store, and suddenly they see Rex the dinosaur in the rearview mirror gaining on them fast. This is an allusion to another movie, *Jurassic Park*. Why did the filmmakers want the audience to think of that movie at that moment?

Point out places where symbols or metaphors are used, and ask students why the author might have chosen that particular reference. What allusion was being made? Why? The allusions should serve to underscore the theme. Therefore, they provide one more set of tools the student can use. As students are summarizing, they can keep track of character traits, point of view, conflicts, and allusions and use these elements to piece together a big-picture understanding of the text as a whole.

Focus: Word Choice

Teachers spend a lot of time telling students not be repetitive in their writing. So why do some authors repeat themselves? That is a good question. Explain to students the importance of emphasis. When an author is repetitive, there must be a good reason. Those words must be very important. Repetition has an impact. Think of the phrases or songs that are burned into our memories because we repeat them so often. Repetition in a narrative is purposeful and should be paid attention to.

In addition to repetition, students should pay attention to the dialogue that is assigned to characters. Just as in argument text, where word choice is determined by the audience and tone, a character's dialogue in a narrative is insight the reader has as to his or her character. Is the dialogue formal? Conversational? Does the character come across as angry? Happy? Young? Old? Through dialogue, we get to know the characters and decide whether we like them. Their likability makes them relatable, and when we can relate to a character, we can put ourselves in his or her shoes and see things from a new perspective. Seeing things through the eyes of a character is one of the most effective ways to promote a theme.

Prerequisite Skills

Because this unit will focus on the reading strategies of summarizing, using text structures, and making connections, students will need practice with these tools. Provide Mini-Lessons on figurative language and literary devices. Provide students with graphic organizers that will help them map out narratives as they read, so they can find a clear beginning, middle, and end. Have them examine character traits, not just to see which characters are "good" and which are "bad," but to understand a character's motivation.

Specific Content-area Vocabulary

Provide specific definitions for each type of point of view (first person, third person, omniscient), and use these academic terms regularly. It is important for students to distinguish between different points of view. Furthermore, establish a common understanding of the difference between quoting a character using the character's dialogue and including a quote from the text to support your ideas. Reinforce the correct punctuation to distinguish the two.

Finally, as students seek and find interesting literary devices, make sure they offer more than just a cursory explanation of why that element was important. Text analysis is difficult and not an innate skill. Students need practice justifying their thinking using evidence from the text as well as inferential information they connected to their own backgrounds. This is where many students will need to start integrating several reading strategies at once—to visualize, ask questions, connect, predict, and infer, so they can finally summarize and generalize a bigger, deeper understanding.

Sample Planning Calendar

Decide on a culminating assignment (some ideas are provided across content areas at the end of this section on page 157). Enter the due date for this project at the end of the third week or the beginning of the fourth week of instruction. Work backward to introduce reading and writing instruction and guided practice opportunities. Allow time for comprehension checks, Mini-Lessons, re-teaching, and test prep. A sample of a four-week unit on narrative writing appears below.

Monday	Tuesday	Wednesday	Thursday	Friday
RI: Story Structure and Elements	RP: Story Structure and Elements	RI: Point of View	RP: Point of View	RI/RP: Character Development
WI: Point of View, Context, Story Structures	WP: Point of View, Context, Story Structures	WI: Character Development V: Descriptive Adjectives	WP: Character Development V: Descriptive Adjectives	WI/WP: Anecdotes G: Past, Present, and Future Tense
RI: Conflict	RP: Conflict WI: Beginning, Middle, and End G: Punctuation, Dialogue	WP: Beginning, Middle, and End WI: Openings and Closings	RI: Summaries WI: Evaluations V: Onomatopoeia	WP: Drafting Culminating Project (optional placement)
WP: Revising Culminating Project (optional placement)	RP: Comprehension Check	WP: Editing G: Verb Agreement TEST PREP	TEST PREP	TEST PREP

Legend

RI = Reading Instruction
RP = Reading Practice
WI = Writing Instruction
WP = Writing Practice
V   = Vocabulary
G   = Grammar

Writing Strategy Overview: Setting the Scene

There are a number of decisions that a student must make before starting a story. Many students get stumped because they don't know what to write about. It is important for these students to use prewriting strategies to help them get lots of ideas on paper. Prewriting gives them interesting choices.

In this section, students use graphic organizers to visually consider the context of setting and point of view. By giving careful consideration to the context of the story, they can understand the circumstances that surround the events and how those circumstances impact the events. Recognizing the point of the view of the storyteller lets students decide to be empathetic or not and personalizes the text to add dimension and activate background knowledge.

The second lesson provides students with a structure for addressing a conflict and then offers a humorous conflict as a way to practice using the structure. This frees students from trying to find an appropriate conflict and spurs their imagination with a creative or humorous topic.

Use these lessons during the prewriting stage of the writing process to get students in a frame of mind for writing and to fill their word banks with rich and varied word choices.

Prewriting Mini-Lesson: Point of View and Context

Common Core State Standard

Engage and orient the reader by establishing a context and point of view and introducing a narrator and/or characters; organize an event sequence that unfolds naturally and logically.

Materials

- Chart paper
- Cardstock
- Pictures of people and locations from magazines
- Reading and Writing Portfolio
- *Character Cards,* page 131
- *Setting Cards,* page 132
- *Who and Where* activity sheet, page 133

Overview

Students will use a graphic organizer to establish a point of view and context for a narrative.

Planning

Before the lesson begins, copy the *Character Cards* and *Setting Cards* onto cardstock and laminate. Then cut as many as is needed for each student to have one.

Procedure

Modeling

1. Tell students that most narratives have a narrator or central character from whose point of view the story is told. Narratives also have specific settings. These two elements work together to help set a context for the story.

2. Show students a picture from a magazine of a person who is playing a particular role, such as a mom or a businessperson.

3. Display the picture. On a sheet of chart paper, draw a small circle in the center, and a larger circle around it. Ask students to label the person in the picture (e.g., businessperson or mom).

4. Ask students to describe the typical characteristics of the person they labeled. They should not be thinking of a *specific* person, just the characteristics of a stereotype of this person. Write students' descriptions in the larger circle, in the area surrounding the small circle.

5. Repeat steps 2 and 3 using a picture of a location. Write students' responses on a second sheet of chart paper.

Guided Practice

6. Have students work with partners. Have each pair choose one *Character Card* and one *Setting Card*.

7. Tell students to make two charts, just like the one modeled on the board. One chart should represent the characteristics of the character, and one should represent the characteristics of the location.

8. Have students share their descriptions.

9. Ask students what kind of situations someone might encounter in the setting that they described.

Independent Practice

10. Tell students that they will work together to write a story using the character they created and the location they described. Distribute copies of the *Who and Where* activity sheets to students.

11. Have students answer the questions on the activity sheet and then write a brief narrative.

Reading Connection

While students read, have them use a note-taking guide that asks them to identify the characters, setting, and situation. Have them stop at the end of each page or after a few paragraphs to clarify this information for themselves. Ask students to use pipe cleaners to create a sculpture that represents their character or one of the situations in the story.

Students can keep a "photo album" of interesting characters in their Reading and Writing Portfolios and add to their albums as they continue reading.

Formative Assessment

If the student...	Consider practicing these prerequisite skills:
had trouble identifying stereotypes	adjectives
had trouble identifying settings	sorting characteristics of different places

Character Cards

Movie star	Tycoon	King	Computer tech
Hero	Tomboy	Loner	Grandma
Cowboy	Southern belle	Athlete	Teenager
Bride	Comic book villain	Salesperson	Artist

The Wild West	A desert island	A big city	A small town
A dark forest	A castle	An undersea kingdom	A spaceship
A farm	A corporate office	A tropical paradise	A small coffee shop
A fancy restaurant	Another planet	A pirate ship	A football stadium

Point of View and Context

Name:_____

Who and Where

Directions: Answer the questions below about your character and setting. Then, use those answers to help you plan and write a short story.

1. What is the name of your character?

2. What is the most important thing about him/her?

3. Where is the setting of your narrative?

4. What is the most important thing to know about this setting?

5. Think of three possible incidents or situations your character could encounter in this setting. List them below.
a.

_____

_____

b.

_____

_____

c.

_____

_____

6. Choose one incident you listed above. On a separate sheet of paper, write a short story about your character using the incident you chose.

Prewriting Mini-Lesson: Conflicts and Events

Common Core State Standard

Write narratives to develop real or imagined experiences or events using effective technique, relevant descriptive details, and well-structured event sequences.

Materials

- Reading and Writing Portfolio
- *Text Types and Purposes Reference Sheet,* page 20
- *Phobia Cards,* page 136
- *Story Map* activity sheet, page 137

Overview

Students will practice establishing and resolving a conflict.

Planning

Introduce the term *conflict,* and be sure students understand it means more than just a fight or a disagreement. In literature, a conflict represents something that the character must overcome, solve, or achieve.

Procedure

Modeling

1. Ask students whether anyone has an allergy. Ask them how their lives are affected by this allergy *(they must avoid cats, peanut butter, or certain medications)*.
2. Tell students that an allergy is something that can't be cured and must be dealt with. In a narrative, a character will have something similar to deal with—maybe not an allergy, but it could be a relative they have to confront, a battle they must fight, or a journey they must take. Regardless of which, there is no option to avoid it in a narrative. The purpose of the narrative is to resolve this situation.
3. Tell students that a narrative uses a specific structure to resolve the conflict. Distribute copies of the *Story Map* activity sheets to students, and display a large version on the board.
4. Explain the narrative structure. Narratives introduce the character and the setting and then introduce the problem. Next, the character experiences several events that lead to the climax. These events usually give the character skills or experiences or teach the character important lessons that will be helpful the when the character reaches the final climax. The climax is where the problem is addressed once and for all. Finally, the story is resolved by showing the consequences of the climax.

Guided Practice

5. Tell students they will work with partners to build a narrative game board. The game board will represent the journey that the character will take and should include tasks or setbacks that the character must encounter.
6. To get started, offer each pair of students one *Phobia Card*. The phobia will be the thing the character must ultimately overcome. Have students use the *Story Map* activity sheet to plan their game boards. Students should include obstacles and rewards for the character, and the setting should offer chances for the character to face his or her fear several times.

Independent Practice

7. Have student pairs write the directions for how to play the game. Ask students to write a narrative description of the game as ad copy for a catalog.

Reading Connection

As students are reading, have them map the events of the narrative on a blank *Story Maps* activity sheet. Encourage students to connect the character's qualities and the unique features of the setting to the events by asking them how these elements affect the events.

Formative Assessment

If the student...	Consider practicing this prerequisite skill:
had trouble identifying the events	sequencing

Fear of… **The color yellow**	*Fear of…* **Peanut butter and jelly sandwiches**	*Fear of…* **Crossing the street**	*Fear of…* **Butterflies**
Fear of… **Toast**	*Fear of…* **Shoelaces**	*Fear of…* **Fish**	*Fear of…* **A bouncing ball**
Fear of… **Malls**	*Fear of…* **Ice cream**	*Fear of…* **Sports**	*Fear of…* **Red lights**
Fear of… **Parties**	*Fear of…* **Spiders**	*Fear of…* **French fries**	*Fear of…* **Country music**

Conflicts and Events

Name:_____

Story Map

Directions: Fill in the map below with the characters, setting, events, climax, and resolution.

Characters:

Setting:

Event 1

Event 2

Event 3

Event 4

Climax

Resolution

Writing Strategy Overview: Adding Dimension

The key to a strong narrative is in the reader's ability to relate to it. This can be accomplished by creating a strong multidimensional character and by building a story that feels universal. A multidimensional character is one who has both good and bad qualities, shows vulnerabilities, and struggles with many of the same problems that we all have. These contradictions within a character make him or her relatable because we all make mistakes and bad decisions and yet still have proud moments of strength and conviction. We all benefit from seeing how someone else who is similar to us responds to stress or anxiety. We are able to empathize and put ourselves in the situation and imagine what we would do. Character development is what hooks the reader into the story because the character becomes a friend whom the reader cares about enough to want to see what will happen next.

What makes a theme universal is its ability to transcend setting. It doesn't matter whether the story takes place in a location we've never visited or even a location that doesn't really exist. As long as we relate to the character, and the situations remind us of similar struggles and challenges we face in our own lives, we will relate to the story no matter where or in what time period it is set. A universal theme represents the big-picture lesson that is learned as a result of resolving a conflict. A story's resolution may teach the character a simple lesson, and that lesson may be one we take to heart as well. But the reader needs to ask himself or herself what the bigger message is that the author is trying to get across. Why was this story the best way to do that? Then the reader will start to have an understanding of the theme.

This section shows how to add dimension to a narrative during the drafting stage of the writing process by creating rich, relatable characters. Then, students will learn how to use allusions and other literary devices to help the reader make connections to his or her own life, other stories, or the world.

Drafting Mini-Lesson: Rich, Relatable Characters

Common Core State Standard

Use narrative techniques, such as dialogue, pacing, and description, to develop experiences, events, and/or characters.

Materials

- Copies of a graphic novel, such as *Storm of the Century* by Stephanie Peters
- Reading and Writing Portfolio
- *Create a Comic Hero* activity sheet, page 141

Overview

Students will add dimension to a character.

Planning

Students can use the computer to add visual images to their *Create a Comic Hero* activity sheet and then print out the results. Then, have them use the activity sheet to build a cube.

Procedure

Modeling

1. Display a page from *Storm of the Century* or another graphic novel and read it aloud for students.
2. Ask students to describe the traits of the character in the comic. Chart their answers and have students sort the responses. After sorting, ask students what kinds of information help them understand a character.
3. Tell students they will create a strong comic character following a simple structure.
4. Distribute copies of the *Create a Comic Hero* activity sheet to students. Read each prompt aloud, and allow time for students to fill in their answers.
5. Ask a few students to share their character sketches. Ask students whether they are able to relate to their classmates' characters. Were there any similarities?
6. Tell students that a character is more memorable when we understand little things about that character, such as what he or she is afraid of, a mistake that haunts him or her, or a particularly proud or funny moment. These are the ways that an author adds dimension to a character.

Guided Practice

7. Have students use their answers from the *Create a Comic Hero* activity sheet to add character information to the cube template.
8. Provide another copy of the *Create a Comic Hero* activity sheet to students. Have students choose a character from a book they are reading or invent a character. Alternatively, students can choose a character from their real lives. Ask students to answer the prompts on the template based on the character they choose. Have students build their cube and work with a partner, taking turns creating characters based on rolling the completed cube and letting the roll determine a detail that must be added to the story.

Independent Practice

9. Ask students to write a comic from the perspective of the character they chose.

10. Have students use a free comic creation website to animate their character, add backgrounds, and tell a story. Students can collaborate to create a league of characters, explaining how they met and what common goal they share.

Reading Connection

While students are reading, have them identify subtle character traits that give them more insight about the character's personality. How does the character react to a fearful situation? How does the character handle loss or accomplishment? Have students highlight the key phrases from the text that help them get a full picture of the character's personality.

Formative Assessment

If the student...	Consider practicing these prerequisite skills:
had trouble identifying character traits	analyzing dialogue for tone
had trouble describing memories	identifying significant details

Rich, Relatable Characters

Name: _____

Create a Comic Hero

Directions: Fill in one detail about the character in each of the cube sides below, or write your own prompts and work with a partner. Take turns creating characters based on rolling the completed character cube.

Draw or insert a picture of the character.	
Describe the character's greatest fear.	Describe the character's childhood home.

What was the character's biggest mistake?	Describe the character's best friend.	

	Describe the character's proudest moment.

Drafting Mini-Lesson: Allusions

Common Core State Standard

Use precise words and phrases, relevant descriptive details, and sensory language to capture the action and convey experiences and events.

Materials

- Chart paper
- Sticky notes
- Reading and Writing Portfolio
- *Explain That Logo* activity sheet, page 144
- *Thematic Ideas Cards,* page 145
- *Tableaus* activity sheet, page 146

Overview

Students will use familiar logos and brands to identify the historical or mythical allusions being portrayed. Then students will use allusions to create tableaus to express a thematic idea.

Planning

Find at least three examples of logos that make use of stories, history, or time periods that are familiar to students, such as Greek mythology, history, or popular culture.

Procedure

Modeling

1. Explain the word *allusion*. Tell students an allusion is an author's way of leading the reader to make a connection. This connection could be to something historical or something going on in the world at the present time. Tell students that authors make allusions because they want the reader to link two events or situations and see the similarities.

2. Attach at least three different logos to sheets of chart paper, and display them on the walls around the room.

3. Have students take turns examining each logo. They will then write their ideas about the allusion being made on a sticky note, initial the note, and post it on the chart.

Guided Practice

4. Discuss the logos with students.

5. Distribute copies of the *Explain That Logo* activity sheet to students. Have students work with partners.

6. Ask students to work together to answer the questions on the activity sheet. Have students share their answers.

7. Have students work with partners or in groups of three or four. Have each group choose one *Thematic Ideas Card,* and distribute copies of the *Tableaus* activity sheet to students. Tell students they will work together to create a tableau that represents the thematic idea indicated on their card. One card is blank for students to select their own thematic idea. Give students about 10 to 15 minutes to discuss and create their tableaus.

8. Have each group of students present its tableau. The other students should guess the thematic idea that each tableau represents and write their responses on their *Tableaus* activity sheets.

Independent Practice

9. Tell students to choose one of the tableaus they saw and write a paragraph that describes the specific elements of that tableau that helped them understand the thematic idea. Their responses should include the vocabulary word *allusion* or *allude*.

10. Have students share their paragraphs. Discuss any similarities or differences among students' responses. Point out that allusions are most effective when a majority of people can relate to them.

Reading Connection

Finding allusions in reading can be challenging. Have students keep a running list of places, objects, or specific descriptions used in a text they are reading. As they are summarizing the story, have them look at the list they compiled. Is there anything on their list that makes them think of something historical, topical, or from popular culture? Remind students to consider the objects and events on their list in the context of the story. (For example, an elephant may not represent anything if the story is set in a zoo, but if the story is about politics, an elephant would be a strong symbol of the Republican Party.)

Formative Assessment

If the student...	Consider practicing these prerequisite skills:
had trouble identifying thematic traits	stereotypes
had trouble describing allusions	making connections and activating prior knowledge

Allusions

Name:_____

Explain That Logo

Directions: Examine the logos that your teacher has placed around the room. Then answer the questions below.

Describe the logo:

To what is the logo alluding?

Why would the logo make this allusion? What emotion or feeling is this allusion creating in the reader's mind?

_____

Describe the logo:

To what is the logo alluding?

Why would the logo make this allusion? What emotion or feeling is this allusion creating in the reader's mind?

_____

Describe the logo:

To what is the logo alluding?

Why would the logo make this allusion? What emotion or feeling is this allusion creating in the reader's mind?

Christopher Columbus	Prometheus steals fire from the gods	Going on vacation
Graduation	Winning the big game	First dance
Man lands on the moon	Zombies attack	The *Titanic* sinks
Going off to war	Staying home sick	

Allusions

Name:_____

Tableaus

Directions: As each group presents its tableau, try to guess the thematic idea they are representing. How did you know? Choose one of the tableaus you saw, and write a paragraph describing the elements of that tableau that contributed to your understanding of the thematic idea.

Group 1
Thematic Idea:

_____

I recognized the following elements in the tableau:

_____

_____

_____

These elements made me think of:

_____

_____

_____

Group 2
Thematic Idea:

_____

I recognized the following elements in the tableau:

_____

_____

_____

These elements made me think of:

_____

_____

_____

Tableaus (cont'd.)

Group 3
Thematic Idea:

_____

I recognized the following elements in the tableau:

_____

_____

_____

These elements made me think of:

_____

_____

_____

Group 4
Thematic Idea:

_____

I recognized the following elements in the tableau:

_____

_____

_____

These elements made me think of:

_____

_____

_____

Writing Strategy Overview: Revising

In a narrative, an author is trying to achieve a certain impact upon the reader. There are specific parts of the story that are more important than others, and the author wants the reader to pay particular attention to these details. The author provides emphasis through repetition and voice.

As teachers, we tell our students over and over not to be repetitive. Even in this book, students are taught to choose unique transition words, descriptions, and sentence structures as a way to keep the text interesting for the reader. Savvy students will come across examples of text that are repetitive and wonder why it was acceptable for that author when it has not been acceptable for them.

The answer is that students are still relatively inexperienced with words and all the nuances and subtleties that exist in vocabulary. They need exposure to and practice with as many words as possible. But a seasoned author presumably has lots of experience with words and has a wide vocabulary from which to choose just the right word. For these authors, repetition is a way to provide extra impact. When a word is used multiple times, it sticks in the reader's mind and stands out as more important. When used this way, repetition can be a powerful literary device. Students need practice recognizing when repetition is used effectively and when it is cumbersome.

The other way to add impact is through voice. The author needs to insert his or her voice into the story. Without voice, the narrative is simply a dry recitation of events. The author can be very subtle or overt about how to insert his or her voice. In many ways, voice is what distinguishes a narrative from informational text. In a narrative, the author has license to insert his or her own opinions and offer value judgments. Then it is up to the reader to agree or disagree with the author's perspective.

Revising Mini-Lesson: Repetition

Common Core State Standard

Use precise words and phrases, relevant descriptive details, and sensory language to capture the action and convey experiences and events.

Materials

- Chart paper
- Lyrics to songs in the public domain, such as "Jingle Bells," "You Are My Sunshine," etc.
- *No Repeats, Please!* activity sheet, page 151

Overview

Students will remove repetitive words and phrases from familiar songs and poems and revise the lyrics in order to see the impact that repetition has on meaning.

Planning

Follow this activity by having students revise a piece of text they previously drafted (from their Reading and Writing Portfolios). Ask them to find ways to use repetition purposefully to add emphasis to particular parts of a story.

Procedure

Modeling

1. Display the lyrics to a familiar song (from the public domain). Distribute copies of the lyrics to students.
2. Read the lyrics aloud. As you read, ask students to circle on their own copy any words or phrases that are repeated.
3. Ask students why authors might repeat words or phrases in a song. What effect does the repetition have on the listener?
4. Ask students to tell you what the song is about. Write their ideas on the board.
5. Create a rating scale on a sheet of chart paper. For each word that is repeated, assign it a rating based on its importance to the theme of the song.

Guided Practice

6. Distribute copies of the *No Repeats, Please!* activity sheet to students. Tell students they will see a familiar song on this sheet.
7. Have students circle all the words that are repeated. Then, have them list synonyms for the words they chose.
8. Ask students to rewrite the song by substituting a different synonym each time the word is repeated. The goal is to eliminate as many repetitive words as possible.
9. Ask students to share their new version of the song with the replacement words.
10. Which words would the students rate as most important? Have them answer on their activity sheets.

Independent Practice

11. Have students choose a piece of text from their Reading and Writing Portfolios. Tell students to look for examples of words they repeated.

12. Ask students to rate the repeated word according to its importance to the theme.

13. Tell students words that are not important to the theme should not be repeated if at all possible. Have students go through their drafts and replace any low-rated words.

14. Tell students words that are very important or representative of the theme may be repeated for impact. Ask students to reread their drafts and determine which highly rated words deserve repetition.

15. Ask students to write a paragraph justifying their repeated use of a word. Have them attach this paragraph to their final draft.

16. Optional extension: During the revision process, ask students whether there is a specific emotion they are trying to emphasize. What word or phrase portrays that emotion? Have students find ways to stress that emotion by using repetition purposefully to call attention to this word or phrase. Repetition is effective with as few as three repetitive words and phrases. Too much repetition can be cumbersome, but just enough is powerful.

Reading Connection

As students read, have them continue to identify words that are repeated and rate them according to the theme. Ask students whether the repetition made a difference in determining the theme. Have them keep good examples of repetitive words and phrases in their Reading and Writing Portfolios.

Formative Assessment

If the student...	Consider practicing this prerequisite skill:
had trouble thinking of synonyms	thesaurus and dictionary skills

Repetition

Name: _____

No Repeats, Please!

Directions: Circle the words that are repeated in the song below. Use the synonym box below the song to brainstorm replacements for the repeated words. Then rewrite the song using the synonyms you chose.

"Over There"

By George M. Cohan (1917)

Over there, over there, send the word, send the word over there,

That the Yanks are coming, the Yanks are coming,

The drums rum-tumming everywhere.

So prepare, say a prayer, send the word, send the word to beware.

We'll be over, we're coming over,

And we won't come back til it's over over there.

Synonym Box

Rewrite the song on the lines below.

_____

_____

_____

_____

_____

_____

Revising Mini-Lesson: Dialogue and Voice

Common Core State Standard

Use narrative techniques, such as dialogue, pacing, and description, to develop experiences, events, and/or characters.

Materials

- *Raise Your Voice* activity sheet, page 154
- *Adverb Cards,* page 155
- *Describe the Line Cards,* page 156

Overview

Students will practice adding adverbs and adverbial phrases to dialogue to convey a stronger voice for each character. Students will also examine places in their own writing where they can insert their own voice by adding a specific tone or inserting an opinion.

Planning

Copy and laminate the *Adverb Cards* and *Describe the Line Cards* and cut them apart. Make enough cards so that every student has a choice of three or four different cards.

Procedure

Modeling

1. Distribute copies of the *Raise Your Voice* activity sheet to students. Discuss the characters represented on the sheet, and have students draw a picture and write a short description of each character represented.

2. Review adverbs and adverbial phrases. Tell students that these serve to describe *how*. For this exercise, students will use a set of adverbs and adverbial phrases to identify how each character would say a line of dialogue.

Guided Practice

3. Have students work with partners or in groups of three. Distribute one set of *Adverb Cards* and one set of *Describe the Line Cards* to each group.

4. For this game, students will take turns drawing a card from each set. They will say the line on the *Describe the Line Card* as described by the *Adverb Card*. Then they will assign the line to one of the characters on their *Raise Your Voice* activity sheet.

5. If another player disagrees with the dialogue delivery or the character assignment, he or she may challenge the student to defend the answer. The rest of the players will determine whether the defense is acceptable (letting the student win the point) or unacceptable (forcing the student to replace the two cards and forfeit the point).

6. Players continue until all the characters have had dialogue assigned.

Independent Practice

7. Have students revisit a draft from their Reading and Writing Portfolios. Ask students to examine any place where dialogue is included.

8. Have students add an adverb or adverbial phrase to at least three lines of dialogue.

9. If the narrative contains no dialogue, have students count the number of adverbs used to describe either a character or an event.

10. Have students edit or insert adverbs so that there are at least two per paragraph that help influence the overall voice and tone of the narrative.

Reading Connection

As students read, have them identify different voices by reading aloud. Students should practice adding expression by highlighting the adverbs that describe the dialogue or the situation and then using different tones and different voices to express those perspectives.

Formative Assessment

If the student...	Consider practicing these prerequisite skills:
did not understand one or more of the terms	direct instruction in adverbs
did not change or add to the tone or voice	facts versus opinions

Dialogue and Voice

Name:_____

Raise Your Voice

Directions: Look at the characters named in the boxes below. Draw or insert a picture to represent each character. Then, under each picture, write a short description of each character's personality.

Spoiled little boy	Troublemaker girl
Bakery shop owner	**Farmer**
Banker	**Bad driver**

Sarcastically	Sadly	Angrily
...with an evil laugh	Happily	Crazily
Disgustedly	Ironically	Hopefully
Anxiously	...with a wink	...with a confused expression

"It's nice to meet you."	"I'm having a rough day."	"Life is full of ups and downs."
"When I want something, I'll ask."	"Don't call me that."	"I don't understand."
"That's the funniest thing I've ever heard."	"I am hungry."	"I doubt it."
"Sleep has not come easily."	"It's the truth, I promise."	"I am all out of money."

Culminating Project Ideas

Language Arts

Write a narrative about a challenge you have overcome, a lesson you have learned, or an inspirational person you have known. Create a video, including music and narration, to document your narrative.

Suggested mentor texts: *Little Women* by Louisa May Alcott; *Black Ships Before Troy: The Story of "The Iliad"* by Rosemary Sutcliff; "Oranges" by Gary Soto

Social Studies

Write a social-networking timeline from the perspective of a famous historical figure.

Suggested mentor texts: *Narrative of the Life* of Frederick Douglass: *An American Slave* by Frederick Douglass; *Harriet Tubman: Conductor on the Underground Railroad* by Ann Petry

Mathematics

Write a business proposal for creating a store to sell a new product. Include information about cost of materials, projected sales and actual sales, percentage of sales tax, profit, and percentage of reinvestment funds. Make predictions about any challenges you might face and how you could overcome them.

Suggested mentor text: *The Number Devil: A Mathematical Adventure* by Hans Magnus Enzensberger

Science

Chronicle a week in the life of an organism. Follow the organism through a journey, assign it a quest, or describe a task it must accomplish.

Suggested mentor text: "The Evolution of the Grocery Bag" by Henry Petroski; "Space Probe" from *Astronomy & Space: From the Big Bang to the Big Crunch*, edited by Phillis Englebert

Additional Resources

Essay Frames

I. OPENING PARAGRAPH

Grabber: Use a quote from a narrative (e.g., story, song, poem) that will allow you to discuss literary devices.

_____

_____

_____

_____

Transition to topic: Tell where this quote came from and what it means.

_____

_____

_____

_____

Transition to thesis and main idea: List the devices you chose to explain, and say why you chose these quotes, including whether or not—and why or why not—the literary device is effective

_____

_____

_____

_____

_____

_____

II. BODY PARAGRAPH FRAME

1. **Topic sentence:** Name a literary device used in this narrative, and then tell why it is used. Be sure to include the title and author. For example, "Personification [the device] is used to show sadness [the generalization] in [the piece from which you drew the quote.]"

_____

_____

a. **Describe** the narrative. How long is it? What genre is it?

_____

_____

_____

b. **Explain** what the narrative is about in your own words:

_____

_____

_____

c. **Quote** the line that demonstrates the literary device.

_____

_____

_____

d. **Define** the literary device and tell how this quote is a good example.

_____

_____

_____

_____

2. **Closing sentence:** Use a conclusion word or an adverb to end this paragraph.

_____

_____

_____

HOMEWORK: USE THIS WORKSHEET TO WRITE YOUR BODY PARAGRAPHS, DUE TOMORROW!

III. CLOSING PARAGRAPH

Respond to grabber: Use another quote from the same piece that you used in the opening paragraph.

_____

_____

Explain why this quote goes with the quote you used in the beginning.

_____

_____

Restate the topic.

_____

_____

Restate the thesis and main ideas.

_____

_____

Clincher: What is your last word about this topic? Has your perspective been changed by the narrative? How did the literary devices contribute to your insight?

_____

_____

Title: Use words from your clincher.

_____

Rubric: Point-based

Format – 20 points

Five paragraphs (introduction, three body paragraphs, conclusion)	5
Typed or handwritten in ink	5
Proper paragraphs	5
Spelling/punctuation	5

Opening Paragraph – 25 points

Title matches clincher	5
Quote from a piece; explanation of how the quote is an example of the theme (this is the topic)	7
Topic	3
Thesis	4
Main ideas	6

Body Paragraph – 50 points

Topic sentence	10
Topic sentence names a literary device; topic sentence tells why this device was used	3
Topic sentence names a literary device used in this narrative, tells why it was used, and includes the author and title	2
Explain the narrative (what it is about)	10
Quote a line and explain how this line represents the theme of the piece	10
Explain a literary device that is used (what it is, why it was used, and how it achieves the intended effect.)	10
Closing sentence	3
Use a conclusion word or an adverb to end this paragraph	2

Closing Paragraph – 25 points

Use another quote	6
Restate topic	4
Restate thesis	4
Restate main ideas	6
Clincher	5

Rubric: Analytic

	Above Average (4)	Sufficient (3)	Developing (2)	Needs Improvement (1)
Develops real or imagined experiences or events using effective technique, relevant descriptive details, and well-structured event sequences				
Engages and orients the reader by establishing a context and point of view and introducing a narrator and/or characters; organizes an event sequence that unfolds naturally and logically				
Uses narrative techniques, such as dialogue, pacing, and description, to develop experiences, events, and/or characters				
Uses a variety of transition words, phrases, and clauses to convey sequence and signal shifts from one time frame or setting to another				
Uses precise words and phrases, relevant to descriptive details, and sensory language to capture the action and convey experiences and events				
Provides a conclusion that follows from and reflects on the narrated experiences or events				
Develops and strengthens writing as needed by planning, revising, editing, rewriting, or trying a new approach, focusing on how well purpose and audience have been addressed				
Uses technology, including the Internet, to produce and publish writing; and links to and cites sources				
Draws evidence from literary or informational texts to support analysis, reflection, and research				
Optional: Compares and contrasts a fictional portrayal of a time, place, or character with a historical account of the same period as a means of understanding how authors of fiction use or alter history.				

Rubric: Holistic

4	The theme is easily identified and the reader is engaged by its clear focus and relevant details. Information is presented logically and naturally. There are no more than two mechanical errors or misspelled words to distract the reader.
3	The audience is easily able to identify the theme of the work, which is supported by relevant ideas and supporting details. Information is presented in a logical manner that is easily followed. There is minimal interruption to the work due to misspellings and/or mechanical errors.
2	The audience can identify the central purpose of the student work with little difficulty and supporting ideas are present and clear. The information is presented in an orderly fashion that can be followed with little difficulty. There are some misspellings and/or mechanical errors, but they do not seriously distract from the work.
1	The audience cannot clearly or easily identify the central ideas or purpose of the student work. Information is presented in a disorganized fashion, causing the audience to have difficulty following the author's ideas. There are many misspellings and/or mechanical errors that negatively affect the audience's ability to read the work.

(Adapted from *Assessment: Types of Rubrics*, DePaul University)

Chapter 6

Test Prep

Overview: Dissecting a Prompt

On-demand writing may be one of the most frightening things middle-school students will encounter. They are thrust into a high-stress setting with the pressure of a limited amount of time to write on a subject about which they may be unsure. Many students freeze up, panic, or simply resign themselves to a poor grade.

Purpose

The testing process can make teachers feel impotent. They are unable to help, unable to explain, and unable to show students how to begin. Despite working tirelessly with students in all the steps of the writing process, the on-demand test requires a frenetic synthesis of weeks' and weeks' worth of information.

Teachers should take heart. It's not the writing itself that stymies students. Usually the biggest stumbling block is that they don't know what they're being asked to do. The writing they have done in class has been explicitly described; the sources they have used have been scrupulously analyzed; the rubric has been clear and has outlined exactly what they were to include. On-demand writing gives students none of these assurances.

Fortunately, students can be given strategies that will help them understand what the prompt is asking and guide them as to what they should do first. Students can learn how to use the prompt as their road map to quick organization so that when they start to write, they already have a working rough draft in their heads. If they need to cite from a text that is provided, they can do so confidently because they will know what kind of evidence they are looking for.

The lessons in this section are meant to be taught individually but ultimately practiced as a class as a prewriting exercise, so students gain a flexibility and comfort with the process. The lessons show students how to:

- Determine the task and the purpose of the writing assignment;
- Manipulate the language of the prompt to create their thesis; and
- Use clues from the prompt (either explicit or implied) to sketch out supporting ideas.

Test Prep Strategy: Determine the Task

Focus: Structure and Verbs

Prompts are often structured in a confusing way. In California, the prompts on the writing portion of the California State Tests (CSTs) consist of two paragraphs. Read the (fictional) example below:

> *Think about a time when you have been angry, sad, or lonely. Whom did you turn to? How did you find the motivation to get out of your own head?*

> *Write a letter to your congressman advocating for a program that provides inmates with homeless pets to train and acclimate for adoption. Be sure to use clear examples that support your position.*

Notice how the first paragraph is somewhat descriptive, asking students to reflect on, to ponder, or to imagine something. If students stop reading after the first paragraph of the prompt, they are likely to write about something very different from what the prompt is asking. The second paragraph is where the actual instructions are spelled out. However, the first paragraph can provide some valuable clues about how to structure an effective essay, what kinds of details to include, or the types of arguments that can be used. It is important to give students practice with dissecting prompts so they know what they are being asked to do before they begin writing.

As a caveat, if you plan on providing test prep practice, it is advisable to turn to the released questions from previous years' tests rather than trying to write your own, unless you can successfully mirror the style and format of the actual test. Sometimes a well-meaning teacher can provide a prompt for practice that is not at all similar to what students will actually experience, which can end up being confusing for students and prove counterproductive.

Test Prep Strategy: Create a Thesis

Focus: The Prompt Is the Key

Once students understand what they are being asked, they must quickly create a thesis statement and decide how they will support their claims. This can be difficult under pressure, especially if the prompt centers on a topic about which the students have little experience or knowledge. Again, it is important that students have a plan of action so they don't panic in these situations.

Students need to be shown how to use the information provided in the prompt to create a viable thesis. They don't have to actually have an opinion about the topic. The test is not assessing their conviction; it is assessing their ability to write a cohesive, well-organized essay.

Introduce strategies that allow students to objectively pull their thesis from the prompt and show them how to quickly get started rather than using up valuable time deciding how they feel about the topic.

Focus: Outline Your Ideas

Remember the fictional prompt example from above? While the first paragraph seems superfluous, it can help a student choose the main ideas to support his or her thesis. In that example, the prompt is asking the writer to advocate for a program for inmates to work with animals. The students may or may not have feelings about this topic, but regardless, the first paragraph gives them some help as to how to support their thesis. If the thesis states that inmates should have opportunities to participate in rehabilitative programs, that first paragraph gives two very good reasons why: First, it's hard to stay angry, lonely, or sad when working with an animal; second, helping others is an effective way to stop thinking about your own problems and start on the road to recovery. Each of these reasons could easily become strong supporting ideas for a student's own body paragraphs, and suddenly the student has a viable outline for an essay.

Prerequisite Skills

As you complete each of the units in this resource, consider a few days of test prep around that specific text type, so students experience an immediate application of the skills they will need to proficiently write on demand. After completing the unit on explanatory writing, review with students the types of explanatory writing (process, cause and effect, etc.), types of transition words, and what constitutes a strong supporting detail. Show them how to use their portfolios to help them select a writing structure that is appropriate for the text type. Refer students back to their own work as you introduce the three test prep lessons.

Genre-specific Vocabulary

Teach students the signal words that will indicate the type of essay they will be expected to write. For example, if they are to write an explanatory essay, the prompt will use terms, such as *explain, show, outline, describe how, tell about a process, sequence,* or *describe the steps.* The prompt for an argument might ask students very explicitly to *argue for, convince, persuade,* or *advocate for.* A narrative essay may ask students to *discuss, reveal, share,* or *examine* and will usually involve personal feelings. Unless students have been taught to recognize the signals, they will not be confident about completing the task appropriately.

Writing Strategy Overview: Dissecting the Prompt

Test prep often implies a complete practice test that students can complete without the pressure of accountability. These experiences are helpful for students because they expose students to the time constraints and the testing environment as a dry run. But logistically, it can be a time-consuming process for the teacher. How many days can the teacher devote to test prep in this manner? Realistically, even if a teacher provides three or four opportunities for students to write a practice essay, they are still getting only minimal exposure to the types of questions they may be asked in an actual testing situation.

By breaking down the test prep into smaller pieces, teachers can help students construct a simple series of steps that can be applied to multiple testing situations. If students have a playbook of strategies, they won't feel as stressed when faced with a real testing situation. Moreover, smaller instructional components mean the test prep can be woven into regular instruction more frequently.

In soccer, practice consists of regularly repeating simple drills, combined with authentic application opportunities. These test prep exercises represent the drills, and once students master the processes, the drills can be repeated often as bell work, at stations, for homework, or as extension activities. In this way, students have multiple exposures to the types of questions they will be asked on high-stakes tests and will hopefully experience less trepidation in actual testing situations.

The first test prep exercise has been separated into individual lessons for explanatory/informational, argument, and narrative text types. In this way, the test prep could follow the unit to which it aligns. It is also possible to combine information about all three types of essays in one lesson. All of the lessons follow very similar process steps so that students gain familiarity with the procedure of breaking down a prompt to discern the task and to start planning an appropriate response.

Test Prep Mini-Lesson: Determine the Task

Common Core State Standard

Write informative/explanatory texts to examine a topic and convey ideas, concepts, and information through the selection, organization, and analysis of relevant content.

Materials

- Sample explanatory writing prompts
- Chart paper
- *Dissecting a Prompt Note-Taking Guide,* page 170
- *My Turn Graphic Organizer,* page 171

Overview

Students will brainstorm synonyms for task-oriented words they are likely to find in test prompts and determine how those words can inform the content and structure of an essay. Students will practice distinguishing the verbs in sample prompts that identify and define the tasks. Note: As students become more proficient at this strategy, combine the test prep passages to offer more exposure to various types of essay prompts.

Planning

Find sample prompts from your state test's released questions, or use the items from the Common Core State ELA Standards Appendix B to display and use for student practice. Have prompts that represent various text types. Note: Instead of using note-taking guides and graphic organizers, students can use individual whiteboards to create a graphic organizer or keep the information under a "Test Prep" tab in their Reading and Writing Portfolio. You can also slip the graphic organizer into a sheet protector and have students use wipe-off markers for the guided and independent practice portions of the lesson.

Procedure

Modeling

1. Access students' prior knowledge. Begin by posting a large sheet of chart paper. Write the word *Explain* at the top. Draw a three-column chart on the sheet. Distribute copies of the *Dissecting a Prompt Note-Taking Guide* to students.

2. Think aloud about words that are synonymous with *explain* (for example, *tell, describe,* or *show*). Write the synonymous words in the first column on the chart. Label the column *Verb.* Have students write *Explain* on their note-taking guide on the line labeled "Text Type." Ask students to work with partners to brainstorm additional words and add them to their note-taking guides. Write some of their suggestions on the chart.

3. Label the second column *Means*.... Remind students that an explanatory essay is one in which the author explains *how, why,* or *which.* Write these words in the second column. Then, tell students these words help determine a specific text structure: *how* means the essay will present a process, a sequence, or a series of steps; *why* means the essay will explain a cause and an effect or a problem and a solution; and *which* means the essay will require a comparison. Write these descriptions on the chart paper under the *Means*... column, and have students add these descriptions to their note-taking guides.

4. Label the third column *Plan to Use*…. Remind students that explanatory essays have very specific structures, which means they require specific elements. Write *Transition Words* in the third column, and ask students to supply the types of transition words they remember using for processes, sequences, causes and effects, comparisons, and descriptive or spatial text structures. Add these words to the chart, and have students add them to their note-taking guides.

Guided Practice

5. Distribute copies of the *My Turn Graphic Organizer* to students.
6. Display a sample writing prompt using a document camera or an interactive whiteboard. Highlight or circle the verbs in the prompt. Have students fill in the verbs, in the same order they appear, in the first box of their graphic organizers.
7. Model how to translate the verbs into tasks by referring back to the *Dissecting a Prompt* note-taking guide. For example, if the verb is *describe*, the task is to write an explanatory essay. Ask students to highlight the verb or verbs that identify the actual task the prompt is stating and to articulate the task in the next box on the graphic organizer.
8. Display another prompt, and ask students to work with partners to identify the verbs and then translate them into a task using their note-taking guides as reference.

Independent Practice

9. Have students complete all boxes on the graphic organizer using additional prompts.
10. Ask students to write an explanation of the types of tasks these prompts were describing and to articulate their thinking about how they were able to determine the task. Note: Use sentence frames as necessary to ensure that students are using the appropriate academic vocabulary.
11. Have students turn in their explanations before leaving for the day.

Formative Assessment

If the student...	Consider practicing these prerequisite skills:
struggled with text structures	transition words
struggled with the verbs	synonyms of active verbs

Test Prep

Name: _____

Dissecting a Prompt Note-Taking Guide

Directions: Fill in the chart below.

_____
(Text Type)

Verb	Means...	Plan to use...

Test Prep

Name: _____

My Turn Graphic Organizer

Directions: Read the sample prompt. Highlight or circle the verbs. Then fill in the chart below.

Verbs:
Task:
Because of the verb(s) _____, **this essay is a(n)** _____ essay. **Therefore, I will plan to use** _____ **in my essay.**
Task:
Verbs:
Because of the verb(s) _____, **this essay is a(n)** _____ essay. **Therefore, I will plan to use** _____ **in my essay.**

Test Prep Mini-Lesson: Determine the Task (Argument)

Common Core State Standard

Write arguments to support claims with clear reasons and relevant evidence.

Materials

- Sample argument writing prompts
- Chart paper
- *Dissecting a Prompt Note-Taking Guide,* page 170
- *My Turn Graphic Organizer,* page 171

Overview

Students will brainstorm synonyms for task-oriented words they are likely to find in test prompts and determine how those words can inform the content and structure of an essay. Students will practice distinguishing the verbs in sample prompts that identify and define the tasks.

Planning

Find sample prompts from your state test's released questions, or use the items from the Common Core State ELA Standards Appendix B to display and use for student practice. Have prompts that represent various text types. Note: Instead of using note-taking guides and graphic organizers, students can use individual whiteboards to create a graphic organizer or keep the information under a "Test Prep" tab in their Reading and Writing Portfolio. You can also slip the graphic organizer into a sheet protector and have students use wipe-off markers for the guided and independent practice portions of the lesson.

Procedure

Modeling

1. Access students' prior knowledge. Begin, by posting a large sheet of chart paper. Write *Argument* on the sheet. Draw a three-column chart on the sheet. Distribute copies of the *Dissecting a Prompt Note-Taking Guide* to students.

2. Think aloud about words that are synonymous with *persuade* (for example, *convince, argue for*). Write the synonymous words in the first column on the chart. Label the column *Verb*. Have students write *Argument* on their note-taking guide on the line labeled "Text Type." Ask students to work with partners to brainstorm additional words and add them to their note-taking guides. Write some of their suggestions on the chart.

3. Label the second column on the poster *Means*.... Tell students that an argumentative essay will require the writer to present reasons, both emotional and logical, that will convince an audience of a particular point of view or position. Write this description on the chart paper under the *Means...* column, and have students label the column and add this description to their note-taking guides.

4. Label the third column *Plan to Use*.... Remind students that argument essays also have very specific characteristics. Write *Audience, Tone, and Types of Appeals* in the third column. Ask students to supply types of audiences (*peers, authority*), tones (*formal, casual, angry*), and appeals (*emotional, logical, ethical*) that they remember using for arguments. Add these words to the chart, and have students add them to their note-taking guides.

Guided Practice

5. Distribute copies of the *My Turn Graphic Organizer* to students.

6. Display a sample writing prompt using a document camera or an interactive whiteboard. Highlight or circle the verbs in the prompt. Have students fill in the verbs, in the same order that they appear, in the first box on their graphic organizers.

7. Model how to translate the verbs into tasks by referring back to the *Dissecting a Prompt Note-Taking Guide.* Ask students to highlight the verb or verbs in the prompt that identify the task to complete and to articulate the task in the next box on the graphic organizer.

8. Display another prompt, and ask students to work with partners to identify the verbs and then translate them into tasks using their note-taking guides as reference.

Independent Practice

9. Have students complete all boxes on the graphic organizer using additional prompts.

10. Ask students to write an explanation of the types of tasks these prompts were describing and to articulate their thinking about how they were able to determine the task. Note: Use sentence frames as necessary to ensure that students are using the appropriate academic vocabulary.

11. Have students turn in their explanations before leaving for the day.

Formative Assessment

If the student...	Consider practicing these prerequisite skills:
struggled with persuasive techniques	emotional, logical, and ethical appeals
struggled with tone	audience, point of view, and purpose
struggled with word choice	infinitive verbs and cohesive language

Test Prep Mini-Lesson: Determine the Task (Narrative)

Common Core State Standard

Write narratives to develop real or imagined experiences or events using effective technique, relevant descriptive details, and well-structured event sequences.

Materials

- Sample narrative writing prompts
- Chart paper
- *Dissecting a Prompt Note-Taking Guide,* page 170
- *My Turn* Graphic Organizer, page 171

Overview

Students will brainstorm synonyms for task-oriented words they are likely to find in test prompts and determine how those words inform the content and structure of an essay. Students will practice distinguishing the verbs in sample prompts that identify and define the tasks.

Planning

Find sample prompts from your state test's released questions, or use the items from the Common Core State ELA Standards Appendix B to display and use for student practice. Have prompts that represent various text types. Note: Instead of using note-taking guides and graphic organizers, students can use individual whiteboards to create a graphic organizer or keep the information under a "Test Prep" tab in their Reading and Writing Portfolio. You can also slip the graphic organizer into a sheet protector and have students use wipe-off markers for the guided and independent practice portions of the lesson.

Procedure

Modeling

1. Access students' prior knowledge. Begin by posting a large sheet of chart paper. Draw a three-column chart. Distribute copies of the *Dissecting a Prompt Note-Taking Guide* to students.

2. Think aloud about words that are synonymous with *narrate* (for example, *describe, discuss, tell about a time*..., or *show*). Write the synonymous words in the first column on the chart. Have students write *Narrate* on their note-taking guide on the line labeled "Text Type." Ask students to work with partners to brainstorm additional words and add them to their note-taking guides. Write some of their suggestions on the chart.

3. Label the second column on the poster *Means*.... Remind students that a narrative essay will require the writer to reveal a lesson learned, a challenge that was overcome, or an influential person or event that altered the writer's perspective. Write this description on the chart paper under the *Means*... column, and have students label the column and add this description to their note-taking guides.

4. Label the third column *Plan to Use*.... Remind students that narrative essays may have unusual structures, but they still have some common characteristics. Write *Beginning, Middle, and End* in the third column. Ask students to describe how a narrative (biography or story) might begin (*by introducing the characters, the setting, and the conflict*), what might happen in the middle (*the rising action, the events that lead to the climax*), and what might happen in the end (*the resolution*). Add these descriptions to the chart, and have students add them to their note-taking guides.

Guided Practice

5. Distribute copies of the *My Turn Graphic Organizer* to students.
6. Display a sample writing prompt using a document camera or an interactive whiteboard. Highlight or circle the verbs in the prompt. Have students fill in the verbs, in the same order that they appear, in the first box on their graphic organizers.
7. Model how to translate the verbs into tasks by referring back to the *Dissecting a Prompt Note-Taking Guide*. Ask students to highlight the verb or verbs that identify the actual task in the prompt and to articulate the task in the next box on the graphic organizer.
8. Display another prompt, and ask students to work with partners to identify the verbs and then translate them into tasks using their note-taking guides as reference.

Independent Practice

9. Have students complete all boxes on the graphic organizer using additional prompts.
10. Ask students to write an explanation of the types of tasks these prompts were describing and to articulate their thinking about how they were able to determine the task. Note: Use sentence frames as necessary to ensure that students are using the appropriate academic vocabulary.
11. Have students turn in their explanations before leaving for the day.

Formative Assessment

If the student...	Consider practicing these prerequisite skills:
struggled with sequencing	transition words, timelines, descriptive text structures
struggled with theme	plot structures

Test Prep Mini-Lesson: Create a Thesis (Explanatory/Informational)

Common Core State Standard

Introduce a topic or thesis statement clearly, previewing what is to follow; organize ideas, concepts, and information using strategies such as definition, classification, comparison/contrast, and cause/effect; include formatting (e.g., headings), graphics (e.g., charts, tables), and multimedia when useful to aiding comprehension.

Materials

- Sample explanatory writing prompts
- Highlighters
- *Building a Thesis Graphic Organizer,* pages 178–179

Overview

Students will use information presented in the prompt as the foundation for their thesis statement.

Planning

Find sample prompts from your state test's released questions, or use the items from the Common Core State ELA Standards Appendix B to display and use for student practice. Have prompts that represent various text types. Note: Instead of using note-taking guides and graphic organizers, students can use individual whiteboards to create a graphic organizer or keep the information under a "Test Prep" tab in their Reading and Writing Portfolio. You can also slip the graphic organizer into a sheet protector and have students use wipe-off markers for the guided and independent practice portions of the lesson.

Procedure

Modeling

1. Connect to students' prior knowledge by reminding them of the work they have done in using the verbs in a prompt to identify the task they are being asked to complete. (Have students refer to the independent practice sheets from the previous lesson.) Remind students that a thesis is different from a topic in that it represents the position the author will take about the topic.

2. Distribute copies of the *Building a Thesis Graphic Organizer* to students. Display the sample prompt that appears on students' worksheets. Use a highlighter to call out the verbs in the prompt: *wrote, were headed, deliver, came, communicate, communicate, write, explain, has had, communicate, use, support.* Ask students which verbs identify the task (*write, explain, use*).

3. Underline the nouns surrounding the task verbs (*write* an <u>essay</u>, *explain* the <u>effect</u>, *use* sufficient <u>details</u>). Ask students to underline these nouns on their own sheets and to write the phrases in the "Task" box on their graphic organizers. Have students identify the type of essay this prompt is suggesting *(explanatory, cause and effect).* Model and think aloud: "*Explain the effect* means this will be a cause-and-effect essay."

4. Note that the task directions occur in the second half of the prompt. Tell students that all the information they need to write their thesis is in the prompt.

5. Ask students to identify the topic of the essay. *(The topic is "the effect of technology on communication.")* Have them write the topic on their graphic organizers.

6. Model how to craft the thesis by returning to the prompt. Think aloud as you write on the displayed copy of the graphic organizer: "If I have to *explain the effect*, my thesis must state that technology DID have an effect on communication. That is how I will start my thesis. I will write: *Technology has had a big effect on the way people communicate.*" (Note: As a revision exercise, ask students to restate this thesis in a more creative way, e.g., *Thanks to technology, people have many options for communication.*) Have students write a thesis statement in the "Thesis" box on their graphic organizers.

7. Tell students that a thesis statement should also include an introduction to the supporting ideas that will be presented in the essay. These supporting ideas will make up the topics for the body paragraphs. Typically, an explanatory essay will have two or three supporting paragraphs, which means the student must determine what will be the main ideas of these paragraphs and express them along with the thesis.

8. Tell students the main ideas will most likely come from the prompt. In this case, the body paragraphs should explain at least two ways that technology has affected communication. On the display, use a second color to highlight the following: *hundreds of years ago; a long time to deliver; quicker ways.* Ask students, based on these phrases in the prompt, what one effect technology has had on communication. *(Technology has improved the delivery speed of communication.)* Have students share out and write their responses in the "Main Idea 1" box on their graphic organizers.

9. Use a third color to highlight the following on the display: *people wrote letters; depending on where they were headed; the way people communicate.* Ask students, based on these phrases provided in the prompt: What is another effect that technology has had on communication? *(Technology has impacted tools or forms of communication people use.)* Have students share out and write their responses in the "Main Idea 2" box on their graphic organizers.

Guided Practice

10. Display a new prompt, and have students use the second graphic organizer to fill in the verbs, task, and topic. Have them work with a partner to craft a thesis.

11. Tell students to use two different colors to highlight phrases from the prompt that might indicate two supporting main ideas. Have them share and discuss with a partner.

12. Ask students to write their main ideas on their graphic organizers.

Independent Practice

13. Repeat this process as necessary using new prompts and blank graphic organizers.

Formative Assessment

If the student...	Consider practicing these prerequisite skills:
struggled with identifying the task	active verbs and explanatory text structures
struggled with finding main ideas	creating word webs and identifying synonyms

Test Prep

Name:_____

Building a Thesis Graphic Organizer

Directions: Read the sample prompt below. Highlight the verbs and determine the task. Write the task in the chart below. Identify the topic. Then, craft your thesis and add the topics for the supporting paragraphs.

Hundreds of years ago, people wrote letters to each other. Depending on where they were headed, letters took a long time to deliver. Over the centuries, people came up with quicker ways to communicate.

In the 21st century, people communicate in a number of different ways. Write an essay in which you explain the effect technology has had on the way people communicate. Be sure to use sufficient details to support your ideas.

Verbs:	Task:
Topic:	
Thesis:	
Main Idea 1:	**Main Idea 2:**

Building a Thesis Graphic Organizer (cont'd.)

Directions: Read the sample prompt. Highlight the verbs and determine the task. Write the task in the chart below. Identify the topic. Then, craft your thesis and add the topics for the supporting paragraphs.

Verbs:	Task:
Topic:	
Thesis:	
Main Idea 1:	**Main Idea 2:**

Test Prep Mini-Lesson: Stake Your Claim (Argument)

Common Core State Standard

Introduce claim(s), acknowledge and address alternate or opposing claims, and organize the reasons and evidence logically.

Materials

- Sample argument writing prompts
- Highlighters
- *Building a Claim Graphic Organizer*, pages 182–183

Overview

Students will use information presented in the prompt as the foundation for their claim.

Planning

Find sample prompts from your state test's released questions, or use the items from the Common Core State ELA Standards Appendix B to display and use for student practice. Have prompts that represent various text types. Note: Instead of using note-taking guides and graphic organizers, students can use individual whiteboards to create a graphic organizer or keep the information under a "Test Prep" tab in their Reading and Writing Portfolio. You can also slip the graphic organizer into a sheet protector and have students use wipe-off markers for the guided and independent practice portions of the lesson.

Procedure

Modeling

1. Connect to students' prior knowledge by reminding them of the work they have done in previous lessons using the verbs in a prompt to identify the task they are being asked to complete. (Have students refer to the independent practice sheets from the previous lessons.) Remind students that a claim is different from a topic in that it represents a position or point of view about a topic.

2. Distribute copies of the *Building a Claim Graphic Organizer* to students. Display the sample prompt that appears on students' worksheets. Use a highlighter to call out the verbs in the prompt: *are losing, have, disappears, suffer, choose, is disappearing, explain, be, use, support*. Ask students which verbs identify the task *(choose, explain, use, support)*.

3. Underline the phrases surrounding the task verbs (*choose* **one** resource, *explain* why it needs to be saved, *use* specific reasons and examples, *support* your opinion). Ask students to underline these phrases on their own sheets and to write the phrases in the "Task" box on their graphic organizers. Have students identify the type of essay this prompt is suggesting *(argument)*. Model and think aloud: *"Explain why it needs to be saved* means this essay will need to convince the reader to save one specific resource."

4. Note that the task directions occur in the second half of the prompt. Tell students that all the information they need to state their claim is in the prompt.

5. Ask students to identify the topic of the essay. *(The topic is "one resource that needs to be saved.")* Have them write the topic on their graphic organizers.

6. Model how to craft the thesis by returning to the prompt. Think aloud as you write on the displayed copy of the graphic organizer: "If I have to *choose* **one** resource, my claim must state which resource I want to save. The prompt suggests *forests, animals,* or *clean water.* I could choose one of those resources, or I could choose another. I will choose trees. I will write: *Trees are one resource that should be saved.*" (Note: As a revision exercise, ask students to restate this claim in a more creative way, e.g., *If trees continue to disappear at the current rate, there could be very serious consequences.*) Have students brainstorm some other resources, choose the resource they wish to save, and write a claim in the "Claim" box on their graphic organizers.

7. Tell students that a claim should also include the reasons the author is stating this opinion. These reasons will become the topics for the body paragraphs. Typically, an argument essay will have two or three supporting paragraphs, which means the student must determine what will be the main ideas of these paragraphs and express them along with the claim.

8. Tell students the prompt will likely offer ideas about the kind of evidence to use. In this case, the body paragraphs should explain at least two reasons the student chose a particular resource. On the display, use a different color to highlight the following: *impact on our environment; the environments of other animals and wildlife.* Ask students, based on these phrases, what one reason they could use to explain why a resource should be saved. *(The resource has an impact on the environments of other species.)* Have students share out and write their responses in the "Main Idea 1" box on their graphic organizers.

9. Use a third color to highlight the following on the display: *when one species disappears, many other species suffer.* Ask students, based on these phrases, for another reason that a resource should be saved. *(The disappearance of a species is bad for other species.)* Have students share out and write their responses in the "Main Idea 2" box on their graphic organizers.

Guided Practice

10. Display a new prompt, and have students use the second graphic organizer to fill in the verbs, task, and topic. Have them work with a partner to craft a claim.

11. Tell students to use two different colors to highlight phrases that might indicate two different types of evidence they could find to support their claims. Have them share and discuss with a partner.

12. Ask students to write their main ideas on their graphic organizers.

Independent Practice

13. Repeat this process as necessary using new prompts and blank graphic organizers.

Formative Assessment

If the student...	Consider practicing these prerequisite skills:
struggled with identifying the task	review synonyms and the definition of *persuade*
struggled with choosing evidence	review purpose and audience, and show how those impact tone and word choice

Test Prep

Name: _____

Building a Claim Graphic Organizer

Directions: Read the sample prompt below. Highlight the verbs and determine the task. Write the task in the chart below. Identify the topic. Then, state your claim and add the main ideas as evidence in supporting paragraphs.

Many parts of the world are losing important natural resources, such as forests, animals, or clean water. These resources have tremendous impact on our environment, as well as the environments of other animals and wildlife. When one species disappears, many other species suffer.

*Choose **one** resource that is disappearing and explain why it needs to be saved. Use specific reasons and examples to support your opinion.*

Verbs:	Task:
Topic:	
Claim:	
Main Idea 1:	**Main Idea 2:**

Building a Claim Graphic Organizer (cont'd.)

Directions: Read the sample prompt. Highlight the verbs and determine the task. Write the task in the chart below. Identify the topic. Then, state your claim and add the main ideas as evidence in supporting paragraphs.

Verbs:	Task:
Topic:	
Claim:	
Main Idea 1:	**Main Idea 2:**

Test Prep Mini-Lesson: Create Context and a Point of View (Narrative)

Common Core State Standard

Engage and orient the reader by establishing a context and point of view and introducing a narrator and/or characters; organize an event sequence that unfolds naturally and logically.

Materials

- Sample narrative writing prompts
- Highlighters
- *Building Context and Point of View* Graphic Organizer, pages 187–188

Overview

Students will use information presented in the prompt to establish context and point of view.

Planning

Find sample prompts from your state test's released questions, or use the items from the Common Core State ELA Standards Appendix B to display and use for student practice. Have prompts that represent various text types. Note: Instead of using note-taking guides and graphic organizers, students can use individual whiteboards to create a graphic organizer or keep the information under a "Test Prep" tab in their Reading and Writing Portfolio. You can also slip the graphic organizer into a sheet protector and have students use wipe-off markers for the guided and independent practice portions of the lesson.

Procedure

Modeling

1. Connect to students' prior knowledge by reminding them of the work they have done in using the verbs in a prompt to identify the task they are being asked to complete. (Have students refer to the independent practice sheets from the previous lesson.) Explain to students that in a narrative the thesis represents the lesson learned and is shaped by the context and point of view.

2. Distribute copies of the *Building Context and Point of View Graphic Organizer* to students. Display the sample prompt that appears on students' worksheets. Use a highlighter to call out the verbs in the prompt: *means, keep trying, stop working, think, worked, were, faced, trying, tell, accomplished, use, support*. Ask students which verbs identify the task *(tell, use)*.

3. Underline the phrases surrounding the task verbs (*tell* about a time when you accomplished a difficult goal, *use* specific examples). Ask students to underline these phrases on their own sheets and to write the phrases in the "Task" box on their graphic organizers. Have students identify the type of essay this prompt is suggesting *(narrative)*. Model and think aloud: "*Tell about a time* means this will be a personal narrative essay."

4. Note that the task directions occur in the second half of the prompt. Tell students that all the information they need to start their narratives is in the prompt.

5. Ask students to identify the topic of the essay. *(The topic is "working hard to achieve a goal.")* Think aloud to model how to decide what goal to choose, e.g., saving enough money to buy a skateboard. Give students a few minutes to brainstorm some ideas. Have them write the topic they choose upon their graphic organizers.

6. Model how to establish a point of view by returning to the prompt. Think aloud as you write on the displayed copy of the graphic organizer: "If I have to *tell about a time,* my point of view must be first person. It will be about me." (Note: If the prompt asked students about another person, e.g., to explain what might motivate someone like Rosa Parks to take a stand against injustice, the point of view might be third person and the context would be historical.)

7. Model how to provide context. Think aloud: "*Context* means I have to provide information about the when, the why, and the where of the situation. I have to create a *beginning* in which I introduce the setting, the people involved, and the conflict. I will write *When I was eight* (tells *when* and *who*), *I had a paper route all summer* (tells *what* happened) *to save up money to buy my own skateboard* (tells *why*)." Next, explain that students will write the thesis of the piece, or lesson learned, based on the context and point of view. (Note: As a revision exercise, ask students to restate this thesis in a more creative way, e.g., *Forty dollars might not seem like a lot of money to some, but for an eight year old, it took me all summer to save up to buy my own skateboard.*) Have students write this thesis statement in the "Point of View and Context" box on their graphic organizers. Remind students that it should establish point of view and context.

8. Tell students that a narrative thesis statement should also include an introduction to the supporting ideas that will be presented in the essay. These supporting main ideas will make up the topics for the body paragraphs. A narrative essay could have any number of body paragraphs, but the structure should include a clear beginning, middle, and end.

Guided Practice

9. Tell students the prompt will often give clues about what to include in the supporting paragraphs. On the display, use a different color to highlight the following: *never stop working for your goals.* The beginning of the narrative must include information about how the student chose his or her goal, why it was important to him or her, and his or her plan to achieve it. For example, in the skateboard example, a student might write, *Ever since I had seen my older brother on his skateboard, I knew I had to have one. I went to the store and saw the one I wanted, but it cost 40 dollars. How would I ever earn that kind of money?* Have students brainstorm and share out some of their responses, and have them add this information to the "Beginning" box on their graphic organizers.

10. On the display, use a different color to highlight the following: *some of the obstacles.* Ask students, based on this phrase, to name one type of information they should include in their narratives. *(Some of the obstacles I had to overcome to reach my goals.)* Have students share out and write their responses in the "Middle" box on their graphic organizers.

11. Use a different color to highlight the following on the display: *What kept you motivated?* Ask students, based on this phrase, for another element that should be included in the middle. *(The ways I was encouraged to continue working.)* Have students brainstorm, share out, and then write their responses in the "Middle" box on their graphic organizers.

12. Finally, tell students the ending of the essay should represent the climax and resolution of the essay. In this case, the ending should explain how the goal was finally achieved and what the student learned about not giving up through this experience. Have students brainstorm and share out. Ask them to write their responses in the "End" box on their graphic organizers.

13. Display a new prompt and have students use the second graphic organizer to fill in the verbs, task, and topic. Have them work with a partner to determine a point of view and a context.

14. Tell students to use different colors to highlight phrases that might indicate what to include in the beginning, middle, and end. Have them share and discuss with a partner.

15. Ask students to write their main ideas on their graphic organizers.

Independent Practice

16. Repeat this process as necessary using new prompts and blank graphic organizers.

Formative Assessment

If the student...	Consider practicing these prerequisite skills:
struggled with conflict	character traits
struggled with beginning, middle, and end	story structure and story elements
struggled with point of view	first- and third-person perspectives

Test Prep

Name: _____

Building Context and Point of View Graphic Organizer

Directions: Read the sample prompt below. Highlight the verbs and determine the task. Write the task in the chart below. Identify the topic. Then, determine your point of view and the context, and add the information you will include in the beginning, middle, and end of the narrative.

The expression "Never, never give up" means to keep trying and never stop working for your goals.

Think about a time when you worked hard to achieve a goal. What were some of the obstacles you faced? What kept you motivated to keep trying? Tell about a time when you accomplished a difficult goal. Use specific examples to support your answer.

Verbs:	Task:

Topic:

Point of View and Context:

Beginning:	Middle:	End:

Building Context and Point of View Graphic Organizer (cont'd.)

Directions: Read the sample prompt. Highlight the verbs and determine the task. Write the task in the chart below. Identify the topic. Then, determine your point of view and the context, and add the information you will include in the beginning, middle, and end of the narrative.

Verbs:	Task:	
Topic:		
Point of View and Context:		
Beginning:	**Middle:**	**End:**

Quick-Reference Writing Guide

	Expository			Persuasive	Narrative	Response to Literature
	Process	Compare/Contrast	Cause & Effect			
PURPOSE	To explain...how	To explain...which (choose)	To explain...why	To convince	To reveal	To react
AUDIENCE	Academic	Academic	Academic	Peer/Academic	Peer/Academic	Academic
SIGNAL WORDS IN THE PROMPT	Explain how..., Put in order..., Show how..., Describe the steps...	Compare..., Decide which..., Choose..., Relate...,	List the causes..., Tell why..., Show why..., Give the reasons... What will happen when...	Convince..., Argue..., Persuade..., Promote..., Defend..., Prove...	Tell about a time when..., Remember a situation when..., Have you ever wanted/felt/wished..., How do you feel about...	Respond to..., React..., Give your reaction/feelings about..., What would you do if...
TRANSITIONS/ LANGUAGE/	First, after, later, soon, until, and then, next, eventually, finally	Also, both, likewise, similarly, as well as, although, even though, instead of, on the other hand, however, despite	As a result, so, because, so that, for this reason, therefore, if...then, thus, since, whenever	It follows, furthermore, moreover, again, consequently, therefore, of course, necessarily, clearly, without a doubt	Later, when, before, then, in a while, another thing, after, as if, I learned, now I know, next time	Another example, just as, in the same way as, reinforced by, underscoring, in addition to
	Specific, clear, descriptive	Analogous, parallel structures	Parallel, logical progressions, clear connections	Active verbs, emotional, impassioned, imperatives, cohesive and thematic adjectives	Emotional, revealing, sensitive, touching, heart-rending, honest, sincere	Specific, descriptive, illustrative, tied to text
TRY THIS GRABBER FOR OPENING	Simile or three questions	Simile or three questions	Statistic or three questions	Three questions	"In the moment" or "sound effect" personal anecdote with a connection to the thesis	Quote from the piece with an analysis that connects to the thesis
WAYS TO SUPPORT THE MAIN IDEA	1. Describe or explain 2. Make a comparison 3. Show cause and effect 4. Make a prediction	1. Describe or explain 2. Show cause and effect 3. Make a prediction 4. Show the relationship	1. Describe or explain 2. Compare 3. Predict 4. Deduce 5. Give personal example or quote a source	1. Describe or explain 2. Compare 3. Show cause and effect 4. Predict 5. Use one or two propaganda techniques	1. Describe or explain 2. Compare or connect 3. Show cause and effect 4. Predict 5. Give personal examples 6. Evaluate/give judgment	1. Quote-Analysis 2. Describe/explain 3. Compare/connect 4. Cause/effect OR literary technique
MOST IMPORTANT THING TO REMEMBER	Be simple and specific: use clear, logical order	Find the relationship; distinguish fact from opinion	Clearly relate one event to the next	Be assertive and sure	Be vulnerable and reflective	Use evidence from the text and always explain why you chose it and what it means

References

ACT (2005). *Crisis at the core: Preparing all students for college and work.* Retrieved from http://www.act.org/research/policymakers/pdf/crisis_report.pdf Feb. 25, 2012.

The Albert Shanker Institute (2011, Spring). A call for common content. *American Educator,* 35(1), 41–45.

Alvermann, D. E. (2002). Effective literacy instruction for adolescents. *Journal of Literacy Research,* 34. 189-208. doi: 10.1207/s15548430jlr3402_4.

Allington, R., & Gabriel, R. (2012, March). Every child, every day. *Educational Leadership,* 15(1), 10–15.

Aud, S., Hussar, W., Kena, G., Bianco, K., Frohlich, L., Kemp, J., & Tahan, K. (2011). *The Condition of Education* 2011 (NCES 2011–033). U.S. Department of Education, National Center for Education Statistics. Washington, DC: U.S. Government Printing Office.

Berman, I. (2009). Supporting adolescent literacy achievement. Issue Brief. NGA Center for Best Practices. February 25, 2009. Retrieved from http://carnegie.org/fileadmin/Media/Publications/PDF/0902ADOLESCENTLITERACY.PDF May 20, 2012.

Biancarosa, G. (2012, March). Adolescent literacy: More than remediation. *Educational Leadership,* 15(1), 22–27.

Bitter, C., O'Day, J., Gubbins, P. & Socias, M. (2009): What works to improve student literacy achievement? An examination of instructional practices in a balanced literacy approach. *Journal of Education for Students Placed at Risk* (JESPAR), 14(1). 17-44.

California Department of Education (2012). *Curriculum Frameworks, English Language Arts,* para. 1. Retrieved from http://www.cde.ca.gov/ci/rl/cf/ May 20, 2012.

California State Board of Education (2010, Aug.). *State Board Meeting. Agenda Items* August 2, 2010. Retrieved from www.cde.ca.gov/be/ag/ag/yr10/agenda201008.asp April 18, 2012.

City-Data.com (2009). Retrieved from http://www.city-data.com/school/california-city-middle-ca.html April 15, 2012.

Cohan, George M. "Over There." Leo Feist, Inc., 1917.

Cohle, D. & Towle, W. (2001). *Connecting reading and writing in the intermediate grades: A workshop approach.* Newark, DE: International Reading Association.

Common Core State Standards Implementation Plan for California (2012, March). Retrieved from California Department of Education, Common Core State Standards Resources, http://www.cde.ca.gov/ci/cc/index.asp May 20, 2012.

Common Core State Standards Initiative (2011). Retrieved from http://www.corestandards.org Feb. 26, 2012.

Conley, D.T., Drummond, K.V., de Gonzalez, A., Rooseboom, J., & Stout, O. (2011). Reaching the goal: The applicability and importance of the Common Core State Standards to college and career readiness. Eugene, OR: Educational Policy Improvement Center. Retrieved from https://www.epiconline.org/publications/documents/ReachingtheGoal-FullReport.pdf May 20, 2012.

Cooper, J.D., Kiger, N.D., Robinson, M.D., Slansky, J.A., & Au, K.H. (2011). *Literacy: Helping students construct meaning.* Independence, KY: Cengage Learning.

Cunningham, P.M. & Allington, R.L. (1999). *Classrooms that work: They can all read and write.* New York: Longman.

Cunningham, P., & Hall, D. (2001). *Big blocks grades 4-8. The Four Blocks Literacy Model.* Retrieved from http://www.wfu.edu/education/fourblocks/ Feb. 26, 2012.

DePaul University. (2007). *DePaul Teaching Commons: What Are Rubrics?* Retrieved from http://teachingcommons.depaul.edu/Feedback_Grading/rubrics.html Oct. 16, 2013.

Deshler, D. D. & Hock, M. F. (2006). *Shaping Literacy Achievement.* New York: Guilford Press.

Duke, N. K., Caughlan, S., Juzwik, M. M,. & Martin, N. M. (2012, March). Teaching genre with purpose. *Educational Leadership,* 15(1), 34–39.

Eckert, L. S. (2008). Bridging the pedagogical gap: Intersections between literary and reading theories in secondary and postsecondary literacy instruction. *Journal of Adolescent & Adult Literacy,* 52(2). 110–118.

Franzak, J. (2006, Summer). Zoom: A review of the literature on marginalized adolescent readers, literacy theory, and policy implications. *Review of Educational Research* 76(2). 209–248.

Graham, S. & Hebert, M. (2010). Writing to read: Evidence for how writing can improve reading. *A Report from Carnegie Corporation of New York.* New York: Alliance for Excellent Education.

Graham, S. & Perin, D. (2007). Writing next: Effective strategies to improve writing of adolescents in middle and high schools. *A Report from Carnegie Corporation of New York.* New York: Alliance for Excellent Education.

Guccione, L. M. (2001, May). Integrating literacy and inquiry for English learners. *The Reading Teacher,* 64(8). 567–577.

IRA/NCTE (1996). *Standards for the English Language Arts.* Newark, DE: International Reading Association; Urbana, IL: National Council of Teachers of English.

Mermelstein, L. (2006). Excerpted from *Reading/writing connections in the K–2 classroom: Find the clarity and then blur the lines* (pp. 56–68). Columbus, OH: Allyn & Bacon. Retrieved from http://www.education.com/reference/article/components-balanced-literacy/ February 28, 2012.

Miller, M., & Veatch, N. (2010, Nov.). Teaching literacy in context: Choosing and using instructional strategies. *The Reading Teacher,* 64(3). 154–165.

National Reading Panel. (2000, April). Teaching children to read: An evidence-based assessment of the scientific research literature on reading and its implications for reading instruction. *Report of the National Reading Panel.* U.S. Department of Health and Human Services. Retrieved from http://www.nichd.nih.gov/publications/nrp/smallbook.cfm May 20, 2012.

Partnership for 21st Century Skills (2009). *Framework for 21st Century Learning.* Retrieved from http://www.p21.org/storage/documents/P21_Framework.pdf Feb. 25, 2012.

Partnership for 21st Century Skills. (2011). www.p21.org. May 20, 2012.

Pearlman, B. (2009, Sept.–Oct.). Making 21st century schools. *Educational Technology.* 14-19. Retrieved from http://www.bobpearlman.org/Articles/ET Bob Pearlman article.pdf.

Porter-Magee, K. (2012). Getting Common Core implementation right: the $16 billion question. *Common Core Watch.* Thomas B. Fordham Institute. Retrieved from http://www.edexcellence.net/commentary/education-gadfly-daily/common-core-watch/2012/getting-common-core-implementation-right-the-16-billion-question.html May 20, 2012.

Saulnier, B. (2008). From "Sage on the Stage" to "Guide on the Side" revisited: (Un)Covering the content in the learner-centered information systems course. *Information Systems Education Journal*, 7(60), 1–10.

Swafford, J. & Durrington, V. A. (2010). Middle school students' perceptions: What teachers can do to support reading self-efficacy. *Building literacy communities. Association of literacy educators and researchers yearbook*, Vol. 32. Louisville, KY: Bellarmine University, 221–235.

Sweeny, S. M. (2010, Oct.). Writing for the instant messaging and text messaging generation: Using new literacies to support writing instruction. *Journal of Adolescent & Adult Literacy*, 54(2), 121–130. doi:10.1598/JAAL.54.2.4.

U.S. Department of Education. (1999a). *U.S. Department of Education's 1999 Performance Report and 2001 Annual Plan*. Vol. 1. Retrieved from http://www2.ed.gov/pubs/AnnualPlan2001/index.html May 20, 2012.

U.S. Department of Education. (1999b). *U.S. Department of Education's 1999 Performance Report and 2001 Annual Plan*. Vol. 1. Retrieved from http://www2.ed.gov/pubs/AnnualPlan2001/index.html May 20, 2012.

Vacca, J. L., Vacca, R.T., Gove, M.K., Burkey, L.C., Lenhart, L.A., & McKeon, C. A. (2003). *Reading and learning to read*. Akron, OH: Allyn & Bacon.

Lyon, G. E. (1993). "Where I'm From." *Stories I Ain't Told Nobody Yet*. New York: Theater Communications Group.

Wiggins, G., & McTighe, J. (2008, May). Put understanding first. *Educational Leadership*, 65(8), 36–41.

Wiggins, G., & McTighe, J. (2011). *The Understanding by Design guide to creating high-quality units*. Alexandria, VA: ASCD. Accessed on Understanding by Design® Framework, http://www.ascd.org/ASCD/pdf/siteASCD/publications/UbD_WhitePaper0312.pdf, April 15, 2012.

Wilhelm, J., Baker, T., & Dube, J. (2001). *Strategic reading: Guiding students to life-long literacy*. Portsmouth, NH: Heinemann. Excerpted at http://www.myread.org Feb. 26, 2012.

Wisconsin Department of Public Instruction. "What is the NCLB?" and ten other things parents should know about the No Child Left Behind Act. http://esea.dpi.wi.gov/files/esea/pdf/parents.pdf. Accessed Feb. 25, 2012.